At Issue

Can the War on Terrorism be Won?

Other books in the At Issue series:

At Issue

Can the War on Terrorism be Won?

David Haugen and Susan Musser, Book Editors

GREENHAVEN PRESS

An imprint of Thomson Gale, a part of The Thomson Corporation

THOMSON

GALE

Detroit • New York • San Francisco • New Haven, Conn. • Waterville, Maine • London

THOMSON

GALE

Christine Nasso, *Publisher*
Elizabeth Des Chenes, *Managing Editor*

© 2007 Thomson Gale, a part of The Thomson Corporation.

Thomson and Star logo are trademarks and Gale and Greenhaven Press are registered trademarks used herein under license.

For more information, contact:
Greenhaven Press
27500 Drake Rd.
Farmington Hills, MI 48331-3535
Or you can visit our Internet site at http://www.gale.com

Articles in Greenhaven Press anthologies are often edited for length to meet page require-ments. In addition, original titles of these works are changed to clearly present the main thesis and to explicitly indicate the author's opinion. Every effort is made to ensure that Greenhaven Press accurately reflects the original intent of the authors. Every effort has been made to trace the owners of copyrighted material.

LIBRARY OF CONGRESS CATALOGING-IN-PUBLICATION DATA

Can the War on Terrorism be won? / David Haugen and Susan Musser, book editors.
p. cm. -- (At issue)
Includes bibliographical references and index.
ISBN-13: 978-0-7377-1973-4 (hardcover)
ISBN-13: 978-0-7377-1974-1 (pbk.)
1. Terrorism--United States--Prevention--Juvenile literature. 2. War onTerrorism, 2001--Juvenile literature. I. Haugen, David M., 1969- II. Musser, Susan.
HV6432.C365 2007
973.931--dc22

2006039099

ISBN-10: 0-7377-1973-7 (hardcover)
ISBN-10: 0-7377-1974-5 (pbk.)

Printed in the United States of America
10 9 8 7 6 5 4 3 2 1

Contents

Introduction

On September 11, 2001 nineteen members of the Islamic terrorist group al Qaeda hijacked four jet airliners and turned them into deadly fuel-laden missiles aimed at targets on American soil. Two of the hijacked planes crashed into the twin towers of New York City's World Trade Center while a third was guided into the Pentagon in Washington, D.C. The fourth plane never found its target because the captive passengers decided to fight their hijackers, causing the aircraft to crash into a field in Pennsylvania. In addition to all nineteen terrorists, nearly three thousand people—Americans and foreign visitors—died in the tragic attacks. It was the worst such calamity in recent American history. A total of one thousand Americans had died at the hands of terrorists in the United States and abroad over the three decades prior to 2001, but no single incident had claimed more than five hundred lives. The attacks on September 11 were truly unprecedented.

In response to the devastating terrorist act, the administration of President George W. Bush put America on the offensive, initiating a "War on Terror." The government met with its North Atlantic Treaty Organization (NATO) allies and they jointly declared that the attacks on America were tantamount to attacks on all nineteen members of the alliance. The European nations that constitute NATO began gathering intelligence on terrorist suspects and reporting the movement of known terrorists. Quickly, intelligence networks traced the coordination of the September 11 attacks to Osama bin Laden, a Saudi Arabian dissident who is a suspected founder of al Qaeda and an outspoken opponent of American involvement in the Middle East.

Convinced that Bin Laden was holed up in Afghanistan, the Bush administration demanded that the Taliban government of that nation deliver up the wanted man. The Taliban, an Islamic fundamentalist leadership that was resistant to Western influences and pressure, refused. In October 2001 America and the United Kingdom—with the support of other NATO governments—began a massive air campaign and limited ground war to assist rebel Afghani forces in overthrowing the Taliban. After a month-long advance, the rebel forces captured the majority of Afghanistan's provinces and marched into Kabul, the nation's capital. U.S. special forces aided by loyal Afghani militias then began destroying a succession of al Qaeda strongholds, eliminating al Qaeda resistance but never succeeding in capturing Bin Laden. Although the war in Afghanistan still rages in 2007, the fighting is limited and neither the Taliban insurgents nor al Qaeda operatives coming across the border with Pakistan have succeeded in destabilizing the new government.

After denying al Qaeda a safe haven in Afghanistan to train terrorists, the Bush administration turned its sights upon Iraq. The Muslim nation's leader, Saddam Hussein, had earned U.S. government antipathy for not complying fully with United Nations (UN) inspection teams that were sent to Iraq to guarantee that the nation was not building weapons of mass destruction. Following the 2001 terrorist attacks, the U.S. government announced that the Iraqi threat was compounded by supposed links between Hussein and terrorist organizations. Fearing that Hussein might pass weapons of mass destruction on to al Qaeda or another anti-Western group, the U.S. Congress authorized President Bush in 2002 to use force to compel Hussein to adhere to UN inspection mandates.

On March 20, 2003, the United States, the United Kingdom, Australia, and a coalition of mainly Asian and European nations (though not including many of the large European states that supported the Afghan war) invaded Iraq. The fighting was swift, and by May, Hussein's government was defeated. No weapons of mass destruction were found in Iraq, however, but some argued that evidence of the capacity to build such weapons was uncovered. The war against insurgents in Iraq continues in 2007, bringing increases in U.S. casualties and war weariness at home. The ongoing fighting has also brought the criticism of many nations (including America's allies), which contend that because troops did not locate any weapons of mass destruction, the war had little to do with counterterrorism and much to do with U.S. imperialism.

To the Bush administration and its supporters, the regime changes in both Afghanistan and Iraq were visible victories in the war on terrorism. The president made it clear that nations that sponsored or dealt with terrorists would share the fate of terrorists. As he stated in May 2003, "Any person, organization or government that supports, protects or harbors terrorists is complicit in the murder of the innocent and equally guilty of terrorist crimes. . . . No act of the terrorists will change our purpose, or weaken our resolve, or alter their fate. Their cause is lost; free nations will press on to victory." The sense of accomplishment and optimism, however, was dampened in March 2004 when a series of bomb explosions rocked commuter trains in Madrid, Spain, and killed nearly two hundred people. Authorities eventually linked the terrorist attack to a radical Islamic group from Morocco that supposedly has ties to al Qaeda. Shortly after the attack, the Spanish government changed hands and the new Worker Party leaders acceded to growing antiwar sentiment and pulled Spanish troops out of Iraq. Critics believed that Spain—one of President Bush's "free nations"—was bowing to terrorist pressure.

On July 7, 2005, suicide bombers exploded devices aboard three London subway trains and a public transit bus. The blasts claimed the lives of the bombers and fifty-two civilians. Those responsible for the attacks were said to be acting against Western aggression in the Muslim world, though it remains unclear as to whether the four bombers were affiliated with any known terrorist organizations. Despite another bombing two weeks later that injured no one (as the main explosives failed to detonate), Britain has remained firm in its commitment to fight terrorism. In a September 2005 conference speech, Prime Minister Tony Blair said, "I never doubted after September 11 that our place was alongside America and I don't doubt it now."

Another set of suicide bombings occurred in October 2005 in Bali, Indonesia. Police in Indonesia have no firm evidence to suggest the bombers' motivations or affiliations. They initially assumed the attacks were connected to Jamaah Islamiyah, a terrorist group that conducted bombings in Bali in 2002 and has ties to al Qaeda. Al Qaeda did claim responsibility for the bombings of three hotels in Amman, Jordan, in November 2005, stating that the hotels were frequented by Western diplomats. These and other terrorist acts since 2001 have demonstrated that these clandestine organizations are far from being eradicated. Some observers even suggest that the global war on terror is inciting these acts. In April 2006 portions of the classified National Intelligence Estimate (a document prepared by U.S. intelligence agencies) had a dour analysis of how the Iraq war was proceeding and how terrorist groups were arising in response to what is perceived as a war against Islam in Iraq. One unnamed official told the *New York Times* that the report "says that the Iraq war has made the overall terrorism problem worse."

Whether or not the United States and its allies are winning the war against terrorism is debated in *At Issue: Can the War on Terror Be Won?* Many of the commentators in this anthology focus on America's intent, determination, and capacity to "stay the course," as President Bush has phrased it. The United States is the cornerstone of the war primarily because it was targeted for the most grievous tragedy and because it has had the military and political clout to bring the shadowy war onto large-scale battlefields such as Afghanistan and Iraq. Several nations around the world, however, have continued to support the war for various reasons. Indonesia and the Philippines, for example, remain supportive because Islamic groups have waged insurgency campaigns for years among the island populations. Great Britain, Canada, and Australia have close cultural ties to the United States and have shared economic and diplomatic interests. Many other nations as diverse as Honduras, Thailand, and Denmark have also remained part of what President Bush termed the "coalition of the willing." Holding together this coalition of roughly ninety nations is one of the primary objectives of the United States in the global war on terror because, as Edward V. Badolato, a former member of the U.S. Interagency Group on Terrorism, stated in a 2002 issue of *World & I*, "global coalitions will play a decisive role in the future of U.S. security." Maintaining broad support will likely remain a key asset in the U.S. arsenal as the war continues. Whether it will be enough to ensure victory over terrorism is yet to be seen.

1

Progress in the War on Terror Has Made America Safer

George W. Bush

George W. Bush is the forty-third president of the United States. He won the 2000 election on the Republican ticket and was renominated in 2004. His administration initiated the war on terror after the terrorist attacks against the United States in 2001.

The terrorist attacks of September 11, 2001, taught the U.S. government many lessons on how to protect itself against future tragedies. The country now has better surveillance capabilities to track terrorists, and the many U.S. intelligence and law enforcement agencies are coordinated to manage and disseminate surveillance information. In addition, the newly established Department of Homeland Security is monitoring airlines and other ports of entry to safeguard against possible attacks. Finally, the U.S military is deployed in Afghanistan and Iraq to eliminate regimes that sponsored terrorism and spread democracy to these former hotbeds of extremism.

[Since September 2001], we have waged an unprecedented campaign against terror at home and abroad, and that campaign has succeeded in protecting the homeland. At the same time, we've seen our enemies strike in Britain, Spain, India, Turkey, Russia, Indonesia, Jordan, Israel, Afghanistan, Iraq, and other countries. We've seen that the extremists have not given up on their dreams to strike our nation. Just last month [in August 2006], police and intelligence officers from

George W. Bush, "President Bush Discusses Progress in the Global War on Terror," www.whitehouse.gov, September 7, 2006.

Great Britain, with the help of the United States and other allies, helped break up a terror cell in London. Working together, we foiled a suicide plot to blow up passenger planes on their way to the United States.

Many Americans look at these events and ask the same question: Five years after 9/11 [September 11, 2001], are we safer? The answer is, yes, America is safer. We are safer because we've taken action to protect the homeland. We are safer because we are on offense against our enemies overseas. We're safer because of the skill and sacrifice of the brave Americans who defend our people. Yet five years after 9/11, America still faces determined enemies, and we will not be safe until those enemies are finally defeated.

What Has the United States Done to Protect Itself?

One way to assess whether we're safer is to look at what we have done to fix the problems that the 9/11 attacks revealed. And so today I'll deliver a progress report. The information about the attacks in this report is largely drawn from the work of the 9/11 Commission and other investigations of the terrorist attacks. I'll begin by looking back at four key stages of the 9/11 plot, the gaps in our defenses that each stage exposed, and the ways we've addressed those gaps to make this country safer.

In the first key stage of the 9/11 plot, al Qaeda [terrorist organization] conceived and planned the attacks from abroad. In the summer of 1996, [al Qaeda's leader] Osama bin Laden issued a fatwa from Afghanistan that said this: "by the grace of Allah, a safe base here is now available." And declared war on the United States. A month later, the Taliban [an Islamic fundamentalist group] seized control of Kabul [Afghanistan's capital], and formed an alliance with al Qaeda. The Taliban permitted bin Laden to operate a system of training camps in the country, which ultimately instructed more than 10,000 in terrorist tactics. Bin Laden was also free to cultivate a global financing network that provided money for terrorist operations. With his fellow al Qaeda leaders, Osama bin Laden used his safe haven to prepare a series of attacks on America and on the civilized world.

In order to protect this country, we will keep steady pressure, unrelenting pressure on al Qaeda and its associates.

In August 1998, they carried out their first big strike—the bombing of two U.S. embassies in East Africa, which killed more than 200 people and wounded thousands. Shortly after the embassy bombings, bin Laden approved another attack. This one was called "the planes operation." Our intelligence agencies believe it was suggested by a fellow terrorist named Khalid Sheikh Mohammed—or KSM. KSM's plan was to hijack commercial airliners and to crash them into buildings in the United States. He and bin Laden selected four preliminary targets—the World Trade Center, the Pentagon, the Capitol Building, and the White House. The "planes operation" would become the 9/11 plot—and by the middle of 1999, KSM was at work recruiting suicide operatives to hijack the airplanes.

The first stage of the 9/11 plot exposed serious flaws in America's approach to terrorism. Most important, it showed that by allowing states to give safe haven to terrorist networks that we made a grave mistake. So after 9/11, I set forth a new doctrine: Nations that harbor or support terrorists are equally guilty as the terrorists, and will be held to account. And the Taliban found out what we meant. With Afghan allies, we removed the Taliban from power, and we closed down the al Qaeda training camps. Five years later, Taliban and al Qaeda remnants are desperately trying to retake control of that country. They will fail. They will fail because the Afghan people have tasted freedom. They will fail because their vision is no match for a democracy accountable to its citizens. They will fail because they are no match for the military forces of a free Afghanistan, a NATO [North Atlantic Treaty Organization] Alliance, and the United States of America.

Using All the Tools at America's Disposal

Our offensive against the terrorists includes far more than military might. We use financial tools to make it harder for them to raise money. We're using diplomatic pressure, and our intelligence operations are used to disrupt the day-to-day functions of al Qaeda. Because we're on the offense, it is more difficult for al Qaeda to transfer money through the international banking system. Because we're on the offense, al Qaeda can no longer communicate openly without fear of destruction. And because we're on the offense, al Qaeda can no longer move widely without fearing for their lives.

I learned a lot of lessons on 9/11, and one lesson is this: In order to protect this country, we will keep steady pressure, unrelenting pressure on al Qaeda and its associates. We will deny them safe haven; we will find them and we will bring them to justice.

Key advantages that al Qaeda enjoyed while plotting the 9/11 attack in Afghanistan have been taken away, and so have many of their most important leaders, including Khalid Sheikh Mohammed. For the past three years, KSM has been in the custody of the Central Intelligence Agency [CIA]. He's provided valuable intelligence that has helped us kill or capture al Qaeda terrorists and stop attacks on our nation. I authorized his transfer to Guantanamo Bay [U.S. Navy base in Cuba where suspected terrorists are being detained before trial]— and the sooner the Congress authorizes the military commissions I have called for, the sooner Khalid Sheikh Mohammed will receive the justice he deserves.

Keeping Track of Terrorists

In the second key stage of the 9/11 plot, KSM and bin Laden identified, trained, and deployed operatives to the United

States. According to the 9/11 Commission, two of the first suicide hijackers to join the plot were men named Hazmi and Mihdhar. KSM's plan was to send these two men to infiltrate the United States and train as pilots, so they could fly the hijacked planes into buildings. Both operatives attended a special training camp in Afghanistan, and then traveled to Malaysia and Thailand to prepare for their trip to America. KSM doctored Hazmi's passport to help him enter the United States. And from Thailand, the two men flew to Los Angeles in January 2000. There they began carrying out the plot from inside our nation. They made phone calls to planners of the attack overseas, and they awaited the arrival of the other killers.

Our intelligence community picked up some of this information. CIA analysis saw links between Mihdhar and al Qaeda, and officers tracked Mihdhar to Malaysia. Weeks later, they discovered that he had been accompanied by Hazmi and that Hazmi had flown to Los Angeles. This gave the CIA reason to be suspicious of both these men. Yet, at the time, there was no consolidated terrorist watchlist available to all federal agencies, and state and local governments. So, even though intelligence officers suspected that both men were dangerous, the information was not readily accessible to American law enforcement—and the operatives slipped into our country.

We've improved our ability to monitor and to track and detain [terrorist] operatives before they can strike.

Since 9/11, we've addressed the gaps in our defenses that these operatives exploited. We've upgraded technology; we've added layers of security to correct weaknesses in our immigration and visa systems. Today, visa applicants like Hazmi or Mihdhar would have to appear for face-to-face interviews. They would be fingerprinted and screened against an extensive database of known or suspected terrorists. And when they arrived on American soil, they would be checked again to make sure their fingerprints matched the fingerprints on their visas. Those procedures did not exist before 9/11. With these steps we made it harder for these—people like these guys to infiltrate our country.

Nine-Eleven also revealed the need for a coordinated approach to terrorist watchlists. So we established common criteria for posting terrorists on a consolidated terrorist watchlist that is now widely available across federal, state, and local jurisdictions. Today, intelligence community officials would immediately place terrorist suspects like Hazmi and Mihdhar on a consolidated watchlist—and the information from this list is now accessible at airports, consulates, border crossings, and for state and local law enforcement. By putting terrorists' names on a consolidated watchlist, we've improved our ability to monitor and to track and detain operatives before they can strike.

Another top priority after 9/11 was improving our ability to monitor terrorist communications. Remember I told you the two had made phone calls outside the country. At my direction, the National Security Agency created the Terrorist Surveillance Program. Before 9/11, our intelligence professionals found it difficult to monitor international communications such as those between the al Qaeda operatives secretly in the United States and planners of the 9/11 attacks. The Terrorist Surveillance Program helps protect Americans by allowing us to track terrorist communications, so we can learn about threats like the 9/11 plot before it is too late. . . .

In the third key stage of the 9/11 plot, the rest of the 19 al Qaeda operatives arrived in the United States The first two hijackers in America, Hazmi and Mihdhar, had given up flight training—so Khalid Sheikh Mohammed selected operatives from a cell in Germany to become the new pilots. These men, led by Mohammed Atta, obtained visas and they traveled to the United States, and then they enrolled in flight training schools. Atta and his team visited airports and flight training centers along the East Coast, including here in Georgia. Atta was pulled over by police. On his way—one of his co-conspirators, the terrorist who would go on to pilot Flight 93, was also stopped. Yet there was no information that the men were dangerous, so the officers treated the encounters as routine traffic stops. By September the 10th, the hijackers had moved to their final destinations near major airports and were ready to execute their attack.

As these terrorists finalized their plans, al Qaeda dispatched another operative named Moussaoui to the United States. Moussaoui took flight lessons in Oklahoma and Minnesota, and communicated with an al Qaeda leader abroad. But he remained isolated from the other operatives and was not a suicide hijacker on the day of the attacks, didn't participate in the 9/11 attacks.

The Patriot Act has increased the flow of information within our government and it has helped break up terrorist cells in the United States of America.

During this stage, law enforcement and intelligence authorities failed to share the insights they were learning about the 9/11 plot. For example, an FBI [Federal Bureau of Investigation] intelligence analyst working at the CIA came across information that raised her suspicions about Hazmi and Mihdhar. But she did not relay her concerns to FBI criminal investigators because of a wall—or "the wall" that had developed over the years between law enforcement and intelligence. You see, throughout the government, there was an assumption that law enforcement and intelligence were legally prohibited from sharing vital information. At one point, key officials from the CIA, the intelligence branch of the FBI, the criminal branch of the FBI were all sitting around the same table in New York, but they believed that "the wall" prohibited them from telling each other what they knew about Hazmi and Mihdhar, and so they never put the pieces together. . . .

Coordinating Intelligence

It is clear, after 9/11, something needed to be done to the system, something needed to be changed to protect the American people. And it is clear to me that this started with transforming the FBI to ensure that it would effectively and quickly respond to potential terrorist attacks. And so now the top priority of the FBI, since 9/11—the culture of that important agency, full of decent people, has changed. The top priority is to protect the American people from terrorist attack. The Bureau has hired large numbers of counterterrorism agents and analysts. They're focusing resources on what they need to do to protect America. They created a unified National Security Branch to coordinate terrorist investigations. They expanded the number of Joint Terrorism Task Forces. And the Bureau is submitting more FISA [Foreign Intelligence Surveillance Act] requests in terrorist cases. In other words, they understand the challenge. And the FBI is changing to meet those challenges. The FBI is responding to terrorist threats like Moussaoui more quickly, more effectively, and with more resources. At every level, America's law enforcement officers now have a clear goal—to identify, locate, and stop terrorists before they can kill people.

Since the attacks, we've also worked with Congress to do something about that wall that prevented intelligence and criminal investigators from talking to each other. The wall made no sense. It reflected an old way of thinking. And so I called upon Congress to pass a piece of legislation that would tear down the wall, and that was called the Patriot Act. The Patriot Act has increased the flow of information within our government and it has helped break up terrorist cells in the United States of America. And the United States Congress was right to renew the terrorist act—the Patriot Act. The Terrorist Prevention Act, called the Patriot Act.

We created the National Counterterrorism Center, where law enforcement and intelligence personnel work side-by-side in the same headquarters. This center hosts secure video teleconferences every day that allow for seamless communication among the FBI, the CIA, and other agencies. Now officials with critical threat information are sitting at the same table and sharing information. We created the position of the Director of National Intelligence to operate the intelligence community as a single unified enterprise. We set up the Terrorist Screening Center, which maintains the government's master list of suspected terrorists, and helps get this information in the hands of state and local law enforcement. Today, a police officer who stops a driver for a routine traffic violation can access terrorist watchlists and be automatically directed to the Terrorist Screening Center if there's a match.

We've learned the lessons of September the 11th. We're changing how people can work together. We're modernizing the system. We're working to connect the dots to stop the terrorists from hurting America again.

Securing Airlines

The fourth and final stage of the 9/11 plot came on the morning of the attack. Starting around 6:45 A.M., the 19 hijackers, including Hazmi and Mihdhar, checked in, cleared security, and boarded commercial jets bound for the West Coast. Some of the hijackers were flagged by the passenger pre-screening system. But because the security rules at the time focused on preventing bombs on airplanes, the only precaution required was to hold the operatives' checked baggage until they boarded the airplane. Several hijackers were also carrying small knives or box cutters, and when they reached the security checkpoints, they set off metal detectors. The screeners wanded them, but let them board their planes without verifying what had set off the alarms. When the flights took off, the men hijacked each plane in a similar way—they stabbed or subdued the pilots and crew, they seized control of the cockpit and they started flying the airplane. By 9:03 A.M. the hijackers had driven two of the flights in the World Trade Center. At 9:37 A.M., they had struck the Pentagon. And shortly after 10:00 A.M., the fourth plane crashed into a field in Pennsylvania. The passengers realized what was happening, and they rose up against their captors. These brave passengers saved countless lives on the ground; they likely spared the Capitol or the White House from destruction; and they delivered America its first victory in the war on terror.

We have taken many steps to address the security gaps that the hijackers exploited that morning. We created the Transportation Security Administration to ensure that every passenger and every bag is screened. We increased the number of federal air marshals on domestic and international flights. We trained and authorized thousands of pilots to carry firearms. We hardened cockpit doors to prevent terrorists from gaining access to the controls. We merged 22 government agencies into a single Department of Homeland Security, and tripled spending for homeland security on our airlines, on our ports, and our borders and other critical areas. We will continue to provide the resources necessary to secure this homeland.

Even if all the steps I've outlined this morning had been taken before 9/11, no one can say for sure that we would have prevented the attack. We can say that if America had these reforms in place in 2001, the terrorists would have found it harder to plan and finance their operations, harder to slip into the country undetected, and harder to board the airplanes and take control of the cockpits, and succeed in striking their targets. . . .

On the morning of 9/11, we saw that the terrorists have to be right only once to kill our people, while we have to be right every time to stop them. So we had to make a larger choice about how to respond to the threats to our country. Some suggested that our efforts should be purely defensive, hunkering down behind extreme homeland security and law enforcement measures. Others argue that we should respond overseas, but that our action should be limited to direct retaliation for 9/11. I strongly disagree with both approaches. Nine-Eleven lifted the veil on a threat that is far broader and more dangerous than we saw that morning—an enemy that was not sated by the destruction inflicted that day, and is determined to strike again. To answer this threat and protect our people, we need more than retaliation; we need more than a reaction to the last attack; we need to do everything in our power to stop the next attack.

America on the Offensive

And so America has gone on the offense across the world. And here are some of the results. We've captured or killed many of the most significant al Qaeda members and associates. We've killed al Qaeda's most visible and aggressive leader to emerge after 9/11, the terrorist Zarqawi in Iraq. We've kept the terrorists from achieving their key goal, to overthrow governments across the broader Middle East and to seize control. Instead, the governments they targeted—such as Pakistan and Saudi Arabia—have become some of our most valuable allies in the war on terror. These countries are joined by the largest coalition in the history of warfare—more than 90 nations determined to find the terrorists, to dry up their funds, to stop their plots, and to bring them to justice.

This coalition includes two nations that used to sponsor terror, but now help us fight it—the democratic nations of Afghanistan and Iraq. In Afghanistan, President Karzai's elected government is fighting our common enemies. In showing the courage he's showing, he's inspired millions across the region. In Iraq, Prime Minister Maliki's unity government is fighting al Qaeda and the enemies of Iraq's democracy. They're taking increasing responsibility for the security of their free country.

The war on terror is more than a military conflict—it is the decisive ideological struggle of the 21st century.

The fighting in Iraq has been difficult and it has been bloody, and some say that Iraq is a diversion from the war on terror. The terrorists disagree. Osama bin Laden has proclaimed that the "third world war is raging" in Iraq. Al Qaeda leaders have declared that Baghdad will be the capital of the new caliphate that they wish to establish across the broader Middle East. It's hard to believe that extremists would make large journeys across dangerous borders to endure heavy fighting, and to blow themselves up on the streets of Baghdad for a so-called "diversion." The terrorists know that the outcome in the war on terror will depend on the outcome in Iraq—and so to protect our own citizens, the free world must succeed in Iraq.

As we fight the enemies of a free Iraq, we must also ensure that al Qaeda, its allies and the extremists never get their hands on the tools of mass murder. When we saw the damage the terrorists inflicted on 9/11, our thoughts quickly turned to the devastation that could have been caused with weapons of mass destruction. So we launched the Proliferation Security Initiative—a coalition of more than 70 countries that are cooperating to stop shipments related to deadly weapons. Together with Russia, we're working on a new Global Initiative to Combat Nuclear Terrorism. We worked with Great Britain to persuade Libya to give up its nuclear weapons program, and now the components of that program are secured right here in the United States. We uncovered the black market nuclear network of A.Q. Khan, who was shipping equipment to Iran and North Korea—that network is now out of business. And now the world is uniting to send a clear message to the regime in [the Iranian capital] Tehran: Iran must end its support for terror; it must stop defying its international obligations; and it must not obtain a nuclear weapon. . . .

The war on terror is more than a military conflict—it is the decisive ideological struggle of the 21st century. And we're only in its opening stages. To win this struggle, we have to defeat the ideology of the terrorists with a more hopeful vision. So a central element in our strategy is the freedom agenda. We know from history that free nations are peaceful nations. We know that democracies do not attack each other, and that young people growing up in a free and hopeful society are less likely to fall under the sway of radicalism. And so we're taking the side of democratic leaders and reformers across the Middle East. We're supporting the voices of tolerance and moderation in the Muslim world. We're standing with the mothers and fathers in every culture who want to see their children grow up in a caring and peaceful world. And by leading the cause of freedom in the vital region, we will change the conditions that give rise to radicalism and hatred and terror. We will replace violent dictatorships with peaceful democracies. We'll make America, the Middle East, and the world more secure.

2

America and Its Allies Are Making Progress Against Terrorism in Afghanistan

Harry Heflin

Lieutenant Colonel Harry Heflin is a member of the U.S. Air Force Reserves serving in Afghanistan.

The United States and its coalition allies invaded Afghanistan in October 2001 to root out the terrorist organizations safely harbored by the ruling Taliban regime. Since that time, coalition forces have deposed the Taliban and destroyed the terrorist training camps on Afghan soil. These successful military operations are just part of the coalition's progress in the region. The United States and its allies are continuing to help the Afghan people rebuild their nation, institute democratic reforms, and maintain security from terrorists bent on returning the Taliban to power.

I have been deployed to Afghanistan since April [2005] and occasionally I am asked by friends at home, "Why are we still in Afghanistan?" With all the media attention focused on Iraq [which the United States invaded in 2001], it's easy to understand why someone might ask such a question.

Our presence in Afghanistan is important because we're taking the fight against terrorism directly to the enemy. We are also making a difference in the lives of more than 24 million people by giving them the chance to establish a stable, democratic way of life.

Harry Heflin, "Live from Afghanistan: Forefront of the War on Terrorism," *Officer*, vol. 81, October 2005. Copyright © 2005 Reserve Officers Association of the United States. Reproduced by permission.

The war against terrorism has no distinct battle-lines. Unless the enemy is sought out and destroyed, however, terrorism will continue to spread and threaten the freedom enjoyed by free people throughout the world. The recent terrorist bombings in London [in 2005] and the recent threat against Britain and the United States by al Qaeda's No. 2 man, Ayman-al Zawahri, serve as a stark reminder that the war on terrorism is still with us. We cannot let our guard down because there are those who still wish us and our allies harm. They remain committed to destroying our democratic way of life.

Defeating the Taliban

After the 9/11 terrorist attacks [in September 2001], the United States, with its coalition partners, took the fight directly to the repressive Afghanistan Taliban government and the members of al Qaeda terrorists being given safe haven in Afghanistan. Our intent was simple: to show our resolve to defend the freedoms we hold dear, not only for ourselves but also for the Afghan people. To this day, we continue to wage a counterinsurgency campaign against Taliban remnants and anti-coalition militia. The Afghan National Army is fighting alongside us in many operations. These are Afghan nationals who have stepped forward to serve their country and are being trained by U.S. forces. However, the fight for freedom in Afghanistan is far from over and many challenges remain.

Our military men and women are . . . playing an important part in the development of Afghanistan.

Winning the war on terrorism requires more than winning on the battlefield. The hard work and sacrifices by those who served before us defeated the Taliban and al Qaeda main forces. Their efforts helped set the stage for the election of a new Afghanistan government last fall [in 2004]. Afghan men and women will have gone to the polls to elect provincial representatives September 18 [2005], and for the first time have the chance to elect women representatives. That is saying a lot for people who not so long ago lived under a repressive form of government where women had no rights. It was our military that helped make this possible. That is why we are here!

Nation-Building

The United States and its coalition partners are working diligently to help the people of Afghanistan rebuild their nation. Rebuilding essential social and life support infrastructure is a total team effort. Although not all partners have provided combat troops, they are providing critical services to the Afghan people. For example, the Jordanians and the Egyptians have established hospitals to treat the sick. Many of our partners help by providing security. When the people of Afghanistan feel safe to move about the country, it gives legitimacy to the Afghanistan government and helps foster more growth and development. The Germans, Polish, French, Romanians, Koreans and the list goes on—are filling critical support roles to help the people of Afghanistan.

Our military men and women are also playing an important part in the development of Afghanistan. They use congressionally appropriated funds and work with local civic leaders to identify national and local projects that will have an immediate impact on the health and economic welfare of the Afghan people. These projects address basic physical and safety needs, and help build confidence in the Afghan government.

Whether it is roads that link towns and villages, schools for girls, medical facilities, community water wells, irrigation for agriculture, sanitation, equipment for local police, it is the Afghan people who are giving the blood, sweat, and tears to build a future they can proudly say they built. The Afghan government is still financially dependent on other nations, but I believe that the Afghan people will eventually build a successful, independent economy.

Forty years ago, President [John F.] Kennedy said: "Let every nation know, whether it wishes us well or ill, that we shall pay any price, bear any burden, meet any hardship, support any friend, oppose any foe to assure the survival and the success of liberty. . . ." He said that during the height of the Cold War, but it is just as applicable today in our fight against terror.

3

U.S. Aid Is Helping Win the War Against Terrorism

Andrew Natsios

Andrew Natsios was sworn in on May 1, 2001, as administrator of the U.S Agency for International Development (USAID). Natsios has served previously at USAID, first as director of the Office of Foreign Disaster Assistance from 1989 to 1991 and then as assistant administrator for the Bureau for Food and Humanitarian Assistance (now the Bureau for Humanitarian Response) from 1991 to January 1993.

Winning the war against terrorism will require more than just military might. The United States must contend with the forces that breed terrorism—chiefly poverty, lack of education, and poor governance. America's best weapon in this fight is its economic assistance programs. By providing jobs, building institutions, connecting isolated peoples, improving health care, and generally raising the level of prosperity in impoverished nations, U.S. dollars can help end the despair that prompts many poor foreigners to ally themselves with terrorists who blame the United States for the world's ills. With more opportunities for a better life, few foreigners would choose to join the terrorist cause.

The terrorist attacks of September 11, 2001, and the war on terrorism have brought the most fundamental changes to US security strategy since the beginning of the Cold War. "Defeating terrorism is our nation's primary and immediate priority," stated US President George W. Bush. It is this generation's "calling."

Andrew Natsios, "Fighting Terror with Aid: Underlying Conditions That Foster Terrorism," *Harvard International Review*, vol. 26, fall 2004. Copyright © 2004 The Harvard International Review. Reproduced by permission.

The 2003 National Strategy on Combating Terrorism outlines the US effort against global terror. Its third and fourth objectives—to deny terrorists resources and state sponsorship, and to diminish the underlying conditions that terrorists seek to exploit—are particularly relevant to programs at the US Agency for International Development (USAID). There is a simple reason for the renewed prominence of foreign assistance: the recognition that national security ultimately rests on spreading prosperity and democracy to the rest of the world. Persistent poverty and oppression breed despair. They rob people of their potential and can turn nations into terrorist recruiting grounds. Regimes that are politically and economically closed foment hopelessness and multiply the number of aggrieved, who become easy recruits to the terrorist cause.

The war on terrorism has brought both new urgency and substantial funding increases to USAID's development mission. In 2003, for example, USAID administered a nearly US$14.2 billion portfolio, including supplemental funds for Iraq—up from US$7.8 billion in 2001. With that money, and with the most thorough reassessment of the country's development mission since the end of World War II, we are responding by addressing five conditions besides simple poverty that underlie terrorism: isolation, lack of economic opportunity, weak institutions and governance, lack of financial transparency, and poor educational systems.

Isolation

As the experience of Afghanistan indicates, remote and isolated areas of poorer countries are the most fertile grounds for terrorist fanaticism. These continue to be Taliban [the former ruling party of Afghanistan] strongholds. Road building has been extremely effective in combating isolation. USAID's signal achievement last year was the rehabilitation of the 389-mile-long road connecting Kabul [Afghanistan's capital] with Kandahar—an unprecedented engineering feat given the constricted time frame and insurgency threats. Approximately 35 percent of Afghans live within 50 kilometers of the highway. Plans are being implemented to extend it to Herat, from which it will arc back and reconnect with Kabul. The road is crucial to extending the influence of the new Afghan government, now endowed with democratic legitimacy. When complete, it will help end the isolation that has sheltered the Taliban and fed terrorist insurgency. It will stimulate development and reconnect the country to a larger network of regional trade. Recent evaluations have shown that in places like Nepal, where we built roads decades ago, they have enormously helped to open access to remote areas and counter the impact of insurgent groups.

Countries become vulnerable and subject to terrorist subversion when there are high rates of unemployment.

Radios are another way in which we combat isolation. Afghanistan has a radio culture, and USAID has restored radio transmission towers, it has also funded innovative programming and provided the capital to build private radio stations. For example, Radio Kabul has broken new ground with a program that appeals to the music tastes and concerns of the young, featuring a mix of female and male disk jockeys that is representative of the diverse ethnic groups in Afghan society. Such things were unimaginable under the Taliban. Similarly, USAID recently began funding its "Last Mile" initiative, which will bring rural and isolated populations in the Middle East and elsewhere into the information age via connection to the Internet.

Lack of Economic Growth and Job Creation

Countries become vulnerable and subject to terrorist subversion when there are high rates of unemployment, particularly among males aged 15 to 35. This has been confirmed time and again by our experiences with fragile and failing states. Militias recruit from the ranks of restive, unemployed youths who are easily seduced into the criminal activities that support terrorism.

Our interventions in such countries have focused on quick impact projects that generate employment as they help rebuild communities. In channeling the productive energies of such peoples, these programs also provide visible signs of hope that can counter the call of those who base their appeals on a sense of hopelessness. Indeed, programs such as "food for work" may be the only means of survival for isolated or war-devastated communities. As we found out in Afghanistan, this is what stood between desperation and reliance on Taliban "charity." Another example comes from Mindanao in the Philippines, where USAID has been working to provide economic opportunities and permanent private sector jobs for members of an insurgent group. This prompted another armed group to offer to turn in their guns for a jobs program similar to USAID's in a neighboring village.

The terrorist threat increases when institutions of government and the services they provide have only a tenuous presence.

The most potent weapon against terrorism, however, will come not from external aid but from internal institutional change. We were early supporters of Peruvian economist Hernando De Soto and his efforts in Latin America and Egypt to integrate the marginalized into the mainstream of their nation's economy. USAID is using a wide variety of programs that address the economic isolation imposed by law and custom, tenuous rights to property, regulatory impediments to productive enterprise, and disenfranchisement.

And we apply the lessons from the work of Harvard Business School professor Michael Porter, who contends that for trade agreements to translate into investment, developing countries must have a sound business climate. In much of the developing world, however, it remains difficult to start and run a business. Therefore, USAID has pioneered the "investor roadmap," which examines impediments to investment and business operations in a particular country. We have carried out more than 50 such studies, which provide a basis for working with the host government and private sector to address the most important problems. The roadmap has been hailed by the World Bank as leading the way to the "micro," or firm-level, reform that is increasingly critical to the underdeveloped world.

Weak Institutions and Poor Governance

The terrorist threat increases when institutions of government and the services they provide have only a tenuous presence. Our development programs are committed to building networks of schools and health clinics and seeing that they are competently staffed. In Afghanistan, Iraq, and elsewhere, we are helping the national government implement management systems and modernize key government ministries. Through additional programs, we seek to foster competent political parties, parliaments, local governments, and judicial systems that will ensure the rule of law.

Building and strengthening institutions has been at the center of our efforts in Afghanistan. We are supporting the electoral process and assisting voter registration, political party development, and civic education. We are also expanding our rule of law program to enforce a new constitution and are involved in supporting educational institutions. In almost every country where USAID works—whether we are assisting the Indonesian Attorney General's office in its battle against money laundering or strengthening the rule of law in Colombia—building institutional capacity is central.

Terrorism also breeds in a country where a government is present but gripped by corruption. I have commissioned an USAID-wide anti-corruption strategy. We have supported Transparency International almost from its inception, and we work with a host of related non-governmental organizations in the field. By encouraging publicity and by empowering watchdog groups, we are countering the petty corruption that demoralizes the citizenry and encumbers its activities. The economic drag from such practices is literally incalculable.

In the long term, education is one of our most potent weapons against terrorism.

Weak Financial Systems

Related to weak governance is the issue of weak financial institutions and lack of financial transparency. Of specific significance to the war on terrorism are our efforts to reform banking and financial systems and install auditing practices that will track the monies that serve criminal activities and feed terrorist networks. USAID has helped pass legislation, set up financial crimes investigative groups, and trained bank examiners to identify and report suspicious transactions.

Lack of Education and Training

In the long term, education is one of our most potent weapons against terrorism. We have designed specific programs for the Muslim world that respond to the challenge posed by radical Islam. Radical schools have filled the vacuum in countries like Afghanistan and Pakistan, where the public education system is weak. One approach thus aims to improve the performance of the secular educational system. In addition, USAID shares the view of enlightened Muslims who see the participation of women as key to modernization, and our educational programs are designed accordingly.

Moreover, the very presence of USAID Embassies and Missions in a host country can be a powerful educational force. More than 4,000 Foreign Service Nationals (FSN) work for USAID. I am proud that among the legions of "graduates," both of our educational programs and of our FSN workforce, many have gone on to ministerial posts and other positions of influence in their countries. One FSN graduate, Ana Vilma Albanez de Escobar, was elected as the first female vice president of El Salvador in what was a most promising election for her people and for inter-American relations.

President [George W.] Bush has said the war on terrorism is eminently winnable but will be long and tough. He has also referred to the war as "unconventional," requiring new thinking. He has charged my agency with new challenges and unprecedented responsibilities. I consider it my most important task to respond to this "calling."

4

The UN Is Helping Win the War Against Terrorism

David Cortright

David Cortright is president of the Fourth Freedom Forum, an organization that believes economic and political incentives, not military might, can bring about global peace. Cortright is also a research fellow at the Joan B. Kroc Institute for International Peace Studies at the University of Notre Dame in Indiana. He has served as an adviser to various agencies of the United Nations (UN).

Fighting international terrorism requires the cooperation of many nations. The United Nations, therefore, is the ideal assembly to formulate a global response to terrorism. In the wake of the September 11, 2001 terrorist attacks on the United States, the UN created the Counter-Terrorism Committee (CTC) to share among member states improved methods of combating terrorism and disseminate information on suspected terrorist agents. Since then, UN member states have used the CTC network to freeze financial assets of terrorist organizations and detain and question thousands of terrorist suspects.

The concept of a "war on terror" may be useful as a political metaphor, but defeating [the terrorist organization] Al Qaeda and like-minded groups primarily is a job for international law enforcement. Al Qaeda is not a government that

David Cortright, "Can the UN Battle Terrorism Effectively? Security Council Resolutions Have 'Mobilized States for a Campaign of Nonmilitary Cooperative Law Enforcement Measures to Combat Global Terrorism,'" *USA Today* Magazine, vol. 133, January 2005. Copyright © 2005 Society for the Advancement of Education. Reproduced by permission.

can be subdued by war, but a diverse network of nonstate actors spread across more than 60 countries. Countering such an enemy requires cooperation among many nations. This is a task for which the United Nations is well suited.

Immediately after the Sept. 11, 2001 attacks [against the United States by al Qaeda], the UN Security Council adopted Resolution 1373, which imposed sweeping legal obligations on all 191 UN members. It required every country to freeze the financial assets of terrorists and their supporters, deny them travel or safe haven, prevent terrorist recruitment and weapons supply, and cooperate with other nations in information sharing and criminal prosecution. The resolution mobilized states for a campaign of nonmilitary cooperative law enforcement measures to combat global terrorism.

Creating the Counter-Terrorism Committee

To monitor compliance with these new counterterrorism mandates, Resolution 1373 created the Counter-Terrorism Committee (CTC), which has been described by [former] UN Secretary-General Kofi Annan as the "center of global efforts to fight terrorism." The primary function of the CTC is to strengthen the counterterrorism capacity of UN member states. Its mission, wrote one observer, is to "raise the average level of government performance against terrorism across the globe." The committee serves as a "switchboard," helping to facilitate the provision of technical assistance to those needing help to implement counterterrorism mandates.

[The Counter-Terrorism Committee] has promoted the creation of specialized systems for coordinating global efforts to combat terrorist threats.

The CTC has received high levels of cooperation, but it likewise has faced significant challenges. The committee relies exclusively on reports from member states and has lacked independent means of determining whether countries actually are implementing mandates. Moreover, the committee has been handicapped in its efforts to coordinate the activities of international, regional, and subregional organizations. By early 2004, a consensus emerged in the Security Council on the need to "revitalize" the CTC through the provision of additional resources and authority. These considerations led the Security Council to adopt Resolution 1535 in March 2004, which created a new Counter-Terrorism Executive Directorate (CTED), thus significantly expanding the committee's professional staffing and enhancing its capacity to support implementation.

In April, 2004, the Security Council further strengthened the UN counterterrorism program by adopting Resolution 1540, prohibiting nations from providing any form of support to nonstate actors that attempt to acquire nuclear, chemical, or biological weapons. It mandated a series of enforcement measures that states must execute to prevent such proliferation and established a committee to report on implementation. In October 2004, the Security Council approved Resolution 1566, in response to the school massacre by Chechen separatists at Beslan in North Ossetia, Russia, urging greater cooperation in the fight against terrorism and establishing a working group to consider additional measures. These resolutions demonstrated the council's resolve, but they also created potential overlap with the mission of the CTC and generated uncertainty about how the new bodies will work together.

After nearly three years of operation, the CTC has a record of considerable accomplishment. Most notably, it has promoted the creation of specialized systems for coordinating global efforts to combat terrorist threats. This cooperative approach has helped develop and strengthen international norms.

Concerned Nations Are Cooperating

The committee's attempt to collect information from member states has been highly successful. All 191 submitted first-round reports explaining their efforts to comply with Resolution 1373. The committee's experts responded to these reports by requesting clarifications and more information, which led to additional correspondence and communication. In total, the CTC has received more than 550 reports, making it the repository of what one observer termed "probably the largest body of information about worldwide counterterrorism capacity." The high levels of response confirm the importance most nations attach to compliance. The reports indicate that a number of countries are taking concrete steps to revise their laws and enhance their enforcement capacity.

One of the most objective and reliable indicators of compliance is the increase in the number of countries joining the 12 UN counterterrorism conventions. These provide a basis for nations to cooperate in preventing terrorist financing and carrying out joint law enforcement and intelligence efforts against bombings. In addition, they establish the legal foundation for states to harmonize criminal justice standards and negotiate mutual legal assistance agreements.

Approximately $200,000,000 in potential terrorist funding has been frozen [by UN member states].

The most important of these are the International Convention for the Suppression of Terrorist Bombings and the International Convention for the Suppression of the Financing of Terrorism. Both have witnessed a sharp rise in the rate of ratification since September, 2001. The increase in support for the 10 other UN conventions has been less dramatic, in part because several of these agreements, such as the conventions on air safety, already had broad support before 9/11 [September 11, 2001]. Conventions that address specific areas of terrorist activity (preventing and punishing crimes against internationally protected persons, measures against taking hostages, safeguarding nuclear materials, and marking plastic explosives) have enjoyed a 20–40% increase in the rate of ratification.

In the first four years after the opening of the convention on terrorist bombings, a mere 28 states ratified the agreement. Following Sept. 11, an additional 87 came on-board. In the two years of the convention on terrorist financing, five nations ratified the agreement. Since 9/11, 102 more have signed on.

A majority of UN member states now are working together to coordinate international law enforcement efforts, and deny financing, safe haven, and travel for Al Qaeda and its related terrorist networks. As a result, approximately $200,000,000 in potential terrorist funding has been frozen. Through unilateral, bilateral, and multilateral law enforcement efforts in dozens of countries, more than 4,000 terrorist suspects, including many senior Al Qaeda operatives, have been taken into custody. Although Al Qaeda remains a dangerous and active network and received an inadvertent recruitment boost due to increased anti-American sentiment following the invasion and occupation of Iraq [in 2003], the international counterterrorism program has achieved some success. . . .

Strengthening Regional Security

The CTC has facilitated outreach and coordination among a wide array of specialized agencies and organizations. Attempting to enhance international cooperation always is a formidable task, but the mission of the CTC in this regard truly is herculean. The range of organizations with actual or potential involvement in the UN counterterrorism mission is vast. Every region of the world has a stake in this. Moreover, the resolution mandates touch on a wide range of public activities and affect dozens of specialized agencies.

The CTC has made important strides in encouraging regional organizations to strengthen their capacity. Many have created their own counterterrorism units, especially in Europe, the Asia-Pacific bloc, and Latin America. Some regions are lagging behind, however. The Middle East/North Africa area, for example, has not developed an adequate coordination mechanism to address the full range of counterterrorism priorities. Broader regional coverage is needed in South Asia and in Eastern and Southern Africa as well.

UN declarations and resolutions have been unequivocal in urging strict adherence to human rights standards in the global fight against terrorism.

Improved cooperation is necessary among organizations within the UN system. The CTC has been slow to coordinate with the expert group monitoring implementation of the sanctions against Al Qaeda and the Taliban [the former ruling regime in Afghanistan]. Concerns have been raised about the need for cooperation between the CTC and the committees established pursuant to Resolutions 1540 and 1566. The problem of coordination among these various bodies has not received sufficient attention. There now are four special Security Council bodies working on counterterrorism issues: CTC, the Al Qaeda and Taliban monitoring team, the 1540 committee, and the 1566 working group. While the mandates of these bodies are separate, they do have overlapping duties and responsibilities. The potential for the duplication of efforts under these circumstances is considerable.

Respecting Human Rights

While many of the challenges are procedural, others are more political in nature. Among the most sensitive concerns are those related to the protection of human rights. Controversy has emerged over cases in which individuals have been detained or subjected to financial restrictions without appeal or other due process. In some cases, government officials have used the fight against terrorism as a justification for suppressing longstanding dissident or minority groups, some of which have been advocates of greater democracy and human rights in their nation. More broadly, a number of analysts worry that counterterrorism measures invariably will encroach upon individual and social rights and threaten basic liberties.

UN declarations and resolutions have been unequivocal in urging strict adherence to human rights standards in the global fight against terrorism. As Annan stated in September, 2003: "There is no trade-off to be made between human rights and terrorism. Upholding human rights is not at odds with battling terrorism; on the contrary, the moral vision of human rights—the deep respect for the dignity of each person—is among our most powerful weapons against it. To compromise on the protection of human rights would hand terrorists a victory they cannot achieve on their own. The promotion and protection of human rights . . . should therefore be at the center of anti-terrorism strategies."

At its ministerial meeting in January 2003, the Security Council adopted Resolution 1456, urging greater international compliance with UN counterterrorism mandates, but also reminding states of their duty to respect international legal obligations, "in particular international human rights, refugee and humanitarian law."

A strong case can be made that protecting human rights and strengthening democracy are essential over the long haul in the fight against terrorism. Terrorist movements often arise in societies where civil and human rights are denied and opportunities for political expression are lacking. Protecting human rights and guaranteeing the freedom to voice dissenting views without government interference can help to prevent the rise of political extremism. Nothing will erode support for counterterrorism mechanisms like the CTC more quickly than a perception among ordinary law-abiding citizens that such programs inevitably will compromise basic freedoms.

Challenges Facing the UN Counterterrorism Efforts

The most longstanding and intractable of political challenges facing the CTC is the lack of an agreed definition of terrorism within the United Nations. This conundrum has entangled the UN for four decades. Some countries condemn as terrorism all acts that endanger or take innocent life, while others seek to differentiate what they consider legitimate acts of resistance against oppression. Middle Eastern states in particular have refused to support counterterrorism initiatives that might prejudice Palestinian resistance to the Israeli occupation. It is no accident that ratification of counterterrorism conventions and participation in CTC initiatives are lowest in the Middle East.

Thus far, the CTC has steered clear of these dilemmas by focusing primarily on procedural issues and generic counterterrorism capabilities. It wisely has transcended the differences over competing definitions of terrorism by appealing to the consensus among UN member states that greater efforts are needed to counter the global terrorist threat posed by Al Qaeda. How long the CTC will be able to maintain this balance is subject to much debate.

Another political challenge concerns enforcement. The CTC has decided not to sit in judgment of UN members or to report to the Security Council on those it has determined to be noncompliant. This limits the committee's effectiveness by allowing certain countries to avoid responsibility for taking specific action. If the CTC is to accomplish its mission, this restrained practice will need to be reconsidered. In the present "revitalized" period of UN counterterrorism efforts, the question of what the Security Council should do about states that refuse to implement mandates has become more pressing. Will the council be willing to consider the imposition of sanctions against nations that have received technical assistance, yet still refuse to comply with Resolution 1373? These and other challenges comprise the tasks ahead for UN counterterrorism efforts.

5

America Must Be Prepared for a Long Fight Against Terrorism

Mortimer B. Zuckerman

Mortimer B. Zuckerman is the chairman and editor in chief of U.S. News & World Report *and is the publisher of the* New York Daily News. *He is also the founder and chairman of Boston Properties, Inc.*

Radical Islamic terrorism against the West began well before the notable attacks on America in September 2001. Its rise in recent years is more visibly threatening, but America has always proven capable of meeting military and political challenges. In order to ensure victory, the people of the United States must be prepared to sacrifice—as they have done in previous wars—to see the nation and its values through the undoubtedly long conflict against Islamofascism.

In recent months, public support for America's intervention in Iraq and for the broader war on terrorism has fallen significantly at home. This is a grievous misapprehension of where we are—and where we recognized we were after 9/11 [when al Qaeda terrorists attacked America], when there was broad consensus that the nation was in danger from a new kind of terrorism. The consensus that sustained us then may have proved evanescent, but the fact is there are radicals out there who want to kill us all—any American, men, women,

Mortimer B. Zuckerman, "A Hang-Tough Nation," *U.S. News & World Report*, vol. 139, October 24, 2005. Copyright 2005 U.S. News and World Report, L.P. All rights reserved. Reprinted with permission.

and children. Why? Because in their delusional thinking, they believe Islam provides the justification for it. As one Egyptian commentator put it: "Allah conceived Islam as a religion. Men have transformed it into politics."

The reason this is so difficult for us to understand is that this culture of death is the polar opposite of our culture of life. And it was not created by intervention in Iraq. Iraq may have sharpened the resentments of some radical Islamists and given them a new excuse, but there was no Iraq war in 1993, when they first tried to blow up the World Trade Center, nor before 9/11, when they did blow it up. The attack on the USS *Cole* took place after U.S. forces contributed to the NATO [North Atlantic Treaty Organization]-led operation in Kosovo [in the former Yugoslavia] that saved the lives of many, many Muslims.

The Threat of Islamic Radicalism

The turmoil now roiling the Islamic world is described vividly in an important new book by Tony Blankley, *The West's Last Chance*. The exploding torrent of Muslim energy, something not seen in 500 years, is being fueled by billions of petrodollars coming out of Saudi Arabia in support of an aggressive antiwestern religious teaching called Wahhabism. And it's spreading not just to other Muslim countries but also to the disaffected among the Muslim communities in Europe who can be trained on the Internet in almost every aspect of terrorism.

Nearly 9 in 10 Americans worry, rightly, about the vulnerability of our mass transit systems, our cargo imports at ports and airports, our water supply—indeed, our traditionally free and open society. The Senate Foreign Relations Committee suggests that there is a very high probability (70 percent) of a successful terrorist attack within the next 10 years with weapons of mass destruction, and the very sober former secretary of defense, William Perry, puts the odds of a nuclear attack in the next five years at 50 percent.

Our resolve to fight those responsible for terrorism must be no less than the resolve that we have shown during previous conflicts.

The president [George W. Bush] spoke none too soon in his recent [October 2005] speech emphasizing that Iraq has now become the central front in the war on terrorism and re-stating our larger purposes there. His assertion that we cannot afford to falter, as we have faltered in previous conflicts when the going got tough, is dead-on. Pulling U.S. forces out of Iraq too soon would be the equivalent of rocket fuel for the Is-lamofascists. Iraq would become the new Afghanistan, a safe base from which to launch attacks on us and wage a war against nonradical Muslim governments. And speaking of which, isn't it long past time for Iraq's neighbors to begin condemning the murders of thousands of Muslims in the name of Islam by the Iraqi insurgents?

America Must Not Falter

Our resolve to fight those responsible for terrorism must be no less than the resolve that we have shown during previous conflicts, and we must make the same kind of accommoda-tions in our way of life that we have made in times past. In short, the American people and its leaders must prepare them-selves mentally and emotionally for what is certain to be a long struggle. It is not as if we are without wayposts of suc-cess. Afghanistan, Kuwait, and now Lebanon are all the benefi-ciaries of American resolve.

President Bush has a proper grasp of the nature of the challenge we face. "There's always a temptation in the middle of a long struggle to seek the quiet life," he said recently, "to escape the duties and problems of the world, and to hope the enemy grows weary of fanaticism and tired of murder. . . . But it's not the world we live in."

The president did well to speak forcefully, but his administration has hardly excelled in presenting a steady, coherent case for staying the course in Iraq. For instance, the demoralizing impression has been allowed to ferment that there is only one combat-ready unit of Iraqi troops. In fact, according to Lt. Gen. David Petraeus, an outstanding commander who has been in charge of training Iraqi troops, Iraq now [as of October 2005] has 80 battalions capable of fighting alongside our forces and another 35 that fight with American soldiers embedded in their units. The Iraqi troops showed what they could do at Tal Afar, where a Sunni Arab defense minister, Saadoun Dulaimi, challenged the insurgents. Given that there was virtually a nonexistent Iraqi military force . . . [in early 2004], having 115 units engaged in the battle is a measure of real progress. So is the evolution of Iraqi democracy—witness the recent negotiations among the Sunnis, Shiites, and Kurds that led to . . . elections [in October 2005].

One definition of American genius is lasting five minutes longer than the other side. This is no time to abandon that time-tested virtue.

6

The West Must Prove
Its Values Are Stronger than
Those of Radical Islam

Tony Blair

Tony Blair has served as the prime minister of the United Kingdom since 1997. He has kept Britain a staunch ally of America throughout the war on terror.

Reactionary Islam has set a course to spread its anti-Western ideology throughout the Muslim world. In order for free nations to defeat this threat, democratic people must prove that their values of equality, justice, and tolerance are superior to radical Islam's teachings of hate and vengeance. America, Britain, and the other coalition partners must continue to support moderate, mainstream Islam while persuading young would-be militants that divisiveness and blind fanaticism are not the paths to world peace.

9/11 in the US, 7/7 in the UK, 11/3 in Madrid, the countless terrorist attacks in countries as disparate as Indonesia or Algeria, what is now happening in Afghanistan and in Indonesia, the continuing conflict in Lebanon and Palestine, it is all part of the same thing. What are the values that govern the future of the world? Are they those of tolerance, freedom, respect for difference and diversity or those of reaction, division and hatred? My point is that this war can't be won in a conventional way. It can only be won by showing that our values

Tony Blair, "Speech to the Los Angeles World Affairs Council," www.number-10.gov.uk, August 1, 2006. Reproduced by permission.

are stronger, better and more just, more fair than the alternative. Doing this, however, requires us to change dramatically the focus of our policy.

Unless we re-appraise our strategy, unless we revitalise the broader global agenda on poverty, climate change, trade, and in respect of the Middle East, bend every sinew of our will to making peace between Israel and Palestine, we will not win. And this is a battle we must win.

What is happening today out in the Middle East, in Afghanistan and beyond is an elemental struggle about the values that will shape our future.

A War of Values

It is in part a struggle between what I will call Reactionary Islam and Moderate, Mainstream Islam. But its implications go far wider. We are fighting a war, but not just against terrorism but about how the world should govern itself in the early 21st century, about global values.

The root causes of the current crisis are supremely indicative of this. Ever since September 11th [2001], the US has embarked on a policy of intervention in order to protect its and our future security. Hence Afghanistan. Hence Iraq. Hence the broader Middle East initiative in support of moves towards democracy in the Arab world.

The point about these interventions, however, military and otherwise, is that they were not just about changing regimes but changing the values systems governing the nations concerned. The banner was not actually "regime change" it was "values change".

What we have done therefore in intervening in this way, is far more momentous than possibly we appreciated at the time.

Of course the fanatics, attached to a completely wrong and reactionary view of Islam, had been engaging in terrorism for years before September 11th. In Chechnya, in India and Pakistan, in Algeria, in many other Muslim countries, atrocities were occurring. But we did not feel the impact directly. So we were not bending our eye or our will to it as we should have. We had barely heard of the Taleban [or Taliban, the fundamentalist Islamic ruling party of Afghanistan]. We rather inclined to the view that where there was terrorism, perhaps it was partly the fault of the governments of the countries concerned.

We were in error. In fact, these acts of terrorism were not isolated incidents. They were part of a growing movement. A movement that believed Muslims had departed from their proper faith, were being taken over by Western culture, were being governed treacherously by Muslims complicit in this take-over, whereas the true way to recover not just the true faith, but Muslim confidence and self esteem, was to take on the West and all its works.

You can't defeat a fanatical ideology just by imprisoning or killing its leaders; you have to defeat its ideas.

Reactionary Islam Fights to Save Its Ideology

Sometimes political strategy comes deliberatively, sometimes by instinct. For this movement, it was probably by instinct. It has an ideology, a world-view, it has deep convictions and the determination of the fanatic. It resembles in many ways early revolutionary Communism. It doesn't always need structures and command centres or even explicit communication. It knows what it thinks.

Its strategy in the late 1990s became clear. If they were merely fighting with Islam, they ran the risk that fellow Muslims—being as decent and fair-minded as anyone else—would choose to reject their fanaticism. A battle about Islam was just

Muslim versus Muslim. They realized they had to create a completely different battle in Muslim minds: Muslim versus Western.

This is what September 11th did. Still now, I am amazed at how many people will say, in effect, there is increased terrorism today because we invaded Afghanistan and Iraq. They seem to forget entirely that September 11th predated either. The West didn't attack this movement. We were attacked. Until then we had largely ignored it.

The reason I say our response was even more momentous than it seemed at the time, is this. We could have chosen security as the battleground. But we didn't. We chose values. We said we didn't want another Taleban or a different Saddam [Hussein, the deposed leader of Iraq, executed in 2006]. Rightly, in my view, we realised that you can't defeat a fanatical ideology just by imprisoning or killing its leaders; you have to defeat its ideas.

There is a host of analysis written about mistakes made in Iraq or Afghanistan, much of it with hindsight but some of it with justification. But it all misses one vital point. The moment we decided not to change regime but to change the value system, we made both Iraq and Afghanistan into existential battles for Reactionary Islam. We posed a threat not to their activities simply: but to their values, to the roots of their existence.

We committed ourselves to supporting Moderate, Mainstream Islam. In almost pristine form, the battles in Iraq or Afghanistan became battles between the majority of Muslims in either country who wanted democracy and the minority who realise that this rings the death-knell of their ideology. . . .

The Battle Has Only Begun

Whatever the outward manifestation at any one time—in Lebanon, in Gaza, in Iraq and add to that in Afghanistan, in

Kashmir, in a host of other nations including now some in Africa—[this conflict] is a global fight about global values; it is about modernisation, within Islam and outside of it; it is about whether our value system can be shown to be sufficiently robust, true, principled and appealing that it beats theirs. Islamist extremism's whole strategy is based on a presumed sense of grievance that can motivate people to divide against each other. Our answer has to be a set of values strong enough to unite people with each other.

This is not just about security or military tactics. It is about hearts and minds about inspiring people, persuading them, showing them what our values at their best stand for.

Any time that people are permitted a chance to embrace democracy, they do so.

Just to state it in these terms, is to underline how much we have to do. Convincing our own opinion of the nature of the battle is hard enough. But we then have to empower Moderate, Mainstream Islam to defeat Reactionary Islam. And because so much focus is now, world-wide on this issue, it is becoming itself a kind of surrogate for all the other issues the rest of the world has with the West. In other words, fail on this and across the range, everything gets harder.

Why are we not yet succeeding? Because we are not being bold enough, consistent enough, thorough enough, in fighting for the values we believe in.

We start this battle with some self-evident challenges. Iraq's political process has worked in an extraordinary way. But the continued sectarian bloodshed is appalling: and threatens its progress deeply. In Afghanistan, the Taleban are making a determined effort to return and using the drugs trade as a front. Years of anti-Israeli and therefore anti-American teaching and propaganda has left the Arab street often wildly divorced from the practical politics of their governments. Iran and, to a lesser extent, Syria are a constant source of de-stabilisation and reaction. The purpose of terrorism—whether in Iran, Afghanistan, Lebanon or Palestine—is never just the terrorist act itself. It is to use the act to trigger a chain reaction, to expunge any willingness to negotiate or compromise. Unfortunately it frequently works, as we know from our own experience in Northern Ireland, though thankfully the huge progress made in the last decade there, shows that it can also be overcome.

So, short-term, we can't say we are winning. But, there are many reasons for long-term optimism. Across the Middle East, there is a process of modernisation as well as reaction. It is unnoticed but it is there: in the UAE [United Arab Emirates]; in Bahrain; in Kuwait; in Qatar. In Egypt, there is debate about the speed of change but not about its direction. In Libya and Algeria, there is both greater stability and a gradual but significant opening up.

Most of all, there is one incontrovertible truth that should give us hope. In Iraq, in Afghanistan, and of course in Lebanon, any time that people are permitted a chance to embrace democracy, they do so. The lie—that democracy, the rule of law, human rights are Western concepts, alien to Islam—has been exposed. In countries as disparate as Turkey and Indonesia, there is an emerging strength in Moderate Islam that should greatly encourage us.

7

America Must Confront the Sponsors of Islamic Extremism

Alex Alexiev

An analyst who has worked for the U.S. Department of Defense and the RAND Corporation, Alex Alexiev is currently the vice president for research at the Center for Security Policy in Washington, D.C. The Center for Security Policy is a nonprofit, nonpartisan organization that promotes international peace through American strength.

Radical Islam is gathering strength in Muslim countries across the globe, and many of its adherents are willing to resort to violence to destroy what they believe is the malignancy of Western civilization. So far the United States is committed to fighting radical Islamic terrorism, but it has not been willing to confront the supposedly friendly nations—such as Pakistan and Saudi Arabia—that sponsor terrorists. America will not win the war on terror if it does not contend with its Muslim "allies" that fund and otherwise support terrorism.

On the first week of October, President [George W.] Bush used, for the first time, the term "Islamofascism" to describe the enemy we're facing. In itself, this was a watershed in the War on Terror, but if we want to emerge victorious, we must go beyond rhetoric and directly confront the enemy's ideology, infrastructures, and sponsors.

Alex Alexiev, "What It Takes: If We Are to Win Tthe War on Terror, We Must Do Far More," *National Review*, November 7, 2005. Copyright © 2005 by *National Review*, Inc., 215 Lexington Avenue, New York, NY 10016. Reproduced by permission.

We have done very little of that to date. To be sure, we have taken on al-Qaeda [the terrorist organization responsible for the September 11, 2001, attacks on America], the Taliban [the fundamentalist Islamic former ruling party of Afghanistan], and assorted terrorists, liberated Afghanistan and Iraq, and achieved considerable success in preventing terrorist acts at home. But we have not dealt with the true malignancy at work here. Simply put, it is not [al Qaeda leader] Osama bin Laden who is the problem, but the ideology and infrastructure of extremism that produced him and his ilk. And unlike him, this murderous ideology is not hiding somewhere in a cave, but is spreading rapidly and looks likely to become the dominant idiom in Islam.

The Rise of Extremism

Thirty years ago there was but one state (Saudi Arabia) living under extreme sharia [Muslim law], but today there are half a dozen countries fully or partially governed by that extreme politico-legal system—and several others heading that way. Since 9/11 alone, radical Islamist rule has been consolidated in northern Nigeria, and Bangladesh undermined as a secular democracy by Islamist elements in its own government. In Turkey, [Kemal] Ataturk's secular legacy is being methodically dismantled by Recep Tayyip Erdogan's Islamic regime.

In the West itself, Islamic extremism has made huge strides and dominates the burgeoning Muslim diaspora communities in many European cities. Under Islamist control, they are being transformed into separatist anti-societies that reject Western civilization and its norms. Many are increasingly willing to engage in violence against their fellow citizens. Fully 13 percent of British Muslims, according to a 2004 Home Office survey, approve of terrorism and 1 percent—a staggering 16,000 people—"engaged in terrorist activity at home or abroad, or supported such activity." Earlier German studies indicate that a quarter of Muslim school students are ready to use violence in behalf of Islam.

Islamist ideology would not have been possible without state sponsorship.

Confronted with this onslaught against its most fundamental values, the West has by and large refused to face the reality of this new totalitarian challenge and has instead taken to spouting politically correct platitudes. In the process, we have stubbornly refused to understand the two most salient characteristics of this existential threat to our civilization and the religion of Islam beyond. First, Islamism does not concern religion, but rather sedition and incitement to violence and murder. Second, it is almost always state-sponsored. Unless we grasp these simple facts about the threat we face and act accordingly, there is little hope we will make much lasting progress in the War on Terror.

The West Is the Enemy

Even a perfunctory look at the core beliefs of Islamism—as expressed in the writings of its leading ideologues—is enough to realize that it is our liberal civilization and its norms of freedom, democracy, secularism, and human rights that are the main enemy and target of the Islamofascists. It is these values Islamist sermons in mosques around the world urge Muslims to conduct jihad against and destroy. And those of us who believe in these values, Muslim and non-Muslim alike, *ipso facto* become apostates, deviants, and infidels, a category of subhumans whose blood can readily be spilled.

More disturbing still is that Islamist ideology would not have been possible without state sponsorship—first and foremost, by our "strategic allies," Saudi Arabia and Pakistan. It is

America's strange blind spot about the nefarious role played by these "allies" that presents the greatest threat to dealing with the terrorist challenge.

State Sponsorship

The basic facts of Saudi sponsorship of radical Islam are too well known to require much rehearsal here. According to Riyadh's [capital of Saudi Arabia] own admission, the kingdom has spent an average of no less than $2.5 billion per year for the past three decades [i.e., since the 1970s] to support "Islamic activities." This has allowed it to build and control 210 Islamic centers, 1,500 mosques, 2,000 schools, and 200 colleges in non-Muslim countries alone. As a result, there is hardly a Western city today that does not have an Islamist-controlled institution of one kind or another spewing hatred against the West and Muslims who refuse to submit to radical Islam. It is this infrastructure of extremist mosques, madrassas, "charities," and foundations that was and continues to be the real incubator of fanaticism worldwide and a foe vastly more potent than al-Qaeda.

If democracy is good for Iraq, why is it not good for Pakistan and Saudi Arabia?

While many in Washington now admit the nefarious role played by Riyadh in the past, they seem to believe that, as the kingdom has itself become the target of the terrorist monster it created, it has changed its tune. This is a delusion. The conflict between al-Qaeda's Wahhabis [anti-Western Islamicists] and Saudi Arabia's Wahhabis is more akin to a fight between Mafia clans over turf and spoils than a struggle between ideological rivals. There is no evidence whatsoever that the Saudis have stopped pursuing their subversive Islamist agenda through the dozens of fronts active around the world. Nor is it at all likely that they will do so unless they are forced. The

House of Saud may be fabulously rich and seem all-powerful, but, stripped to its core, it is little more than a clan of corrupt potentates whose sole source of political legitimacy is the reactionary and obscurantist Wahhabi creed.

Pakistani Breeding Grounds

Washington exhibits much the same shortsightedness with respect to our other "strategic ally" in the region, Pakistan. After the London bombings—four years after Islamabad [the capital city of Pakistan] switched sides from being a patron of the Taliban and al-Qaeda to becoming an American ally—President [Pervez] Musharraf admitted that he had, in effect, done nothing to curtail the pervasive jihadist networks and madrassa [Muslim school] hate-factories in his country. He has now made new promises to do that, but there is no reason to believe that it will happen. Indeed, the man charged with carrying out the task, minister of religious affairs Ijaz ul-Haq, recently denied any link between the madrassas and terrorism.

In the meantime, Pakistan remains the premier breeding ground of terrorists; the area bordering Afghanistan continues to be run by Islamists; re-energized Taliban remnants come and go as they please across the frontier; jihadist training camps are in business again in the tribal areas; and our hard-won gains in Afghanistan are at risk. The reason all of this is going on is far from coincidental. We need to realize that there is a deeply synergistic relationship between the Pakistani military and the Islamists, while Musharraf's "alliance" with us is, at best, a marriage of convenience and, at worst, one based on false pretense and duplicity. Musharraf is part of the problem, not the solution.

Going to the Source

What, then, is to be done? The very first thing to do is admit that our policies vis-à-vis Pakistan and Saudi Arabia have been misguided and counterproductive. We might then ask ourselves a simple question: If democracy is good for Iraq, why is it not good for Pakistan and Saudi Arabia? The obvious answer requires that our relations and assistance to these states be made contingent on specific and meaningful steps toward democracy by the current regimes and active U.S. support for democratic alternatives. We should be fully prepared to view these regimes as adversaries. The status quo is simply unacceptable.

At the tactical level, we must immediately start treating Islamists and their networks as those guilty of criminal sedition and incitement to murder ought to be treated. We have abundant proof, for instance, that many Wahhabi international foundations and "charities" have been involved in abetting terrorism. If the Saudis refuse to close them down, we should do so unilaterally by designating them terrorist entities.

The West could also protect itself by enunciating laws that treat inciting violence under the guise of religion as a criminal offense and start putting the Islamists in jail. There are hopeful signs that this may indeed be happening in the United Kingdom, Australia, the Netherlands, and elsewhere. The United States should follow suit by reconsidering its own sedition laws.

The Enlightenment philosopher Denis Diderot once remarked that it is but a step from fanaticism to barbarism. Our best shot at preventing Islamist barbarism is doing everything possible to make sure that there are fewer and fewer fanatics tempted to take that small step. We can make a good start toward that end by going to the source of the Islamist malignancy and by putting some of the fanatics in jail before they have the opportunity to become mass murderers.

8

America Must Rethink the Motivations for Islamic Terrorism

Michal Zapendowski

Michal Zapendowski is a student at Brown University in Providence, Rhode Island.

The United States has a skewed idea that Islamic terrorists are motivated by religious fanaticism and unjust anti-American hatred. In truth, Islamic terrorists see themselves as nationalist freedom fighters hoping to keep the pan-Muslim world free of Western encroachment. It is American support of the Israeli occupation of the holy land as well as U.S. intervention in the Arab world that has drawn the antipathy of Islamic rebels. Until America understands this and tries to repair the gap between the two worlds, the war on terror will likely fail.

Comparing America's imbroglio in Iraq to the Vietnam War has become cliché, but there is another conflict for which the Saigonese simile is far better suited: the war on terror. Insofar as it can be understood as a conflict between two protagonists, the war on terror is clearly a counter-insurgency campaign and in this way it closely resembles the Vietnam War. America fights an insurgent terrorist network that strikes unexpectedly and then recuperates among sympathetic populations.

Understanding what happened in Vietnam is, therefore, key to understanding the war on terror. In a guerrilla war, every citizen is a potential enemy or a potential friend, so each mind you convince is an enemy target destroyed, and each enemy killed is a defeat if it fills two neighboring hearts with anger. This makes conventional military tactics essentially irrelevant. Military force failed in Vietnam because it failed to win the hearts and minds of the Vietnamese populace and thus created a quagmire in which the United States was unable to destroy the insurgency.

In Vietnam, we treated the Vietnamese Communist movement according to our own theories on Communism. We projected a false image onto our enemy, seeing them as nothing but ideological fanatics. Most of the Vietnamese people, on the other hand, saw the VietCong as nationalist freedom fighters fighting an uphill battle against a string of foreign occupiers (Japanese, French and then American).

We're in the midst of making the same mistake in the war on terror. We portray terrorists as religious fanatics, motivated by an irrational ideology of jihad and hatred of freedom. This interpretation reflects the most superficial aspects of the enemy and plays to our own moral superiority complex. It ignores the facts.

The Motivation of Terrorists

There is a distinct division between the religious fanatics who found regimes like the [Afghani] Taliban (bearded mullahs from backwater madrassas [Muslim schools]) and the type of men who run and man terrorist networks. Religious fundamentalists in the Muslim world are primarily concerned with internal enforcement of antiquated moral codes, rarely having the expertise to build a bomb or fly a plane. Our enemy in the war on terror is not ideological Islam.

Islamic terrorists are overwhelmingly the educated sons of middle- and upper-class families. The economic theory of fighting terrorism has got it backwards—terrorism is often the product of wealth and education, rather than poverty and ignorance.

And, as [al Qaeda terrorist leader] Osama bin Laden himself has said, if terrorists organized their attacks because they "hate freedom," they would attack Sweden rather than America and its allies. It is tempting to ignore bin Laden's words due to anger, but his declarations give us insight in this conflict.

We misunderstand Islam by thinking of it merely as a religion.

The true motivations of terrorism are much more prosaic. International terrorism has historically almost always been a form of extreme nationalism. This was true before Serb terrorists assassinated Archduke Franz Ferdinand in 1914, starting World War I, and it remains true after Basque terrorists declared an official end to their campaign in violence in Spain [in 2006]. There was no meaningful ideological element to most international terrorist networks. The issues motivating terrorism are issues of national pride.

The phenomenon of popular nationalism needs to be understood as being especially complex in the Muslim world, where so-called "national" identities are often the results of artificial borders imposed by colonialism, and state-based loyalties intermingle with trans-border identities. Islamic terrorists are religious nationalists, and if they cloak themselves in Islam it is only because Islam is part of their national identity. It is largely because of its intermingling with nationalist identities that Islam has managed to survive, and strengthen itself, in an age when secular nationalism has swept the rest of the world.

Resisting Invasion of the Muslim World

We misunderstand Islam by thinking of it merely as a religion. Like Judaism, Islam is as much a community as it is a faith. Those who once argued that Judaism was a trans-border religion, and therefore could not constitute a nation, were proven wrong by the foundation of Israel. Even though terrorists are not on the verge of founding a pan-Muslim state, it is this religious nationalist frame of reference that constitutes their fundamental motivation. Al-Qaeda grew out of a network of Arab fighters who risked their lives fighting in far-away Afghanistan alongside fellow Muslims. They saw the Soviet invasion of that country in the 1980s as an aggression against a trans-border Muslim nation.

Muslims are effectively second-class citizens in today's world.

Nationalist anger, no matter how unjustified its results, always has root causes. The international issues feeding Muslim and Arab feelings of injustice are many, but the primary issue is the Israeli occupation of the holy sites of East Jerusalem. Both the world's Muslims and the international community reject this occupation, and the selective enforcement of U.N. [United Nations] resolutions that has followed on its heels has served as the kindling to Muslim anger.

Rethinking Muslim Identity

The White House continues to wage its counter-insurgency campaign against an enemy it fundamentally misinterprets. Its appeals to the world's Muslims, neglectful of all major relevant international issues, inevitably fall on closed minds and closed hearts. Forcing Muslim nations to abide by the will of the United Nations while simultaneously refusing to enforce resolutions aimed at protecting their own internationally-recognized rights makes a hollow mockery of the whole international order. Muslims are effectively second-class citizens in today's world. How can we expect Islamic nationalists to lay down their arms when we fail to recognize their rights as equal members of the international community?

The gap between the Muslim world and the rest of the international community is the key to the war on terror and in the battle of hearts and minds, actions carry far more weight than words. Al-Qaeda understands this, it's time that we did as well.

9

Detention of Prisoners at Guantanamo Bay Undermines the War on Terror

USA Today

USA Today is an American daily newspaper published by the Gannett Corporation. It has the largest circulation of any newspaper in the United States.

If America intends to show the world that it can win the war on terror by virtue of the strength of its values, then something must be done about the unlawful detention of Muslim prisoners in Guantanamo Bay, Cuba. The U.S. prison at Guantanamo is holding several hundred unidentified captives taken mainly during the conflict in Afghanistan, and word has leaked out that some of these detainees may have been the victims of abuse by U.S. interrogators. In order to prove that America abides by international codes of conduct regarding prisoners, the government should begin telling the public and the world more about the captives and their treatment.

To understand the raging debate over the future of the U.S. prison camp at Guantanamo Bay, Cuba, consider the tales of two detainees.

- Mohamed al-Kahtani is a Saudi who authorities say was involved in the 9/11 [September 11, 2001] hijacking plot. Interrogation of al-Kahtani and others at Guantanamo has provided information about al-Qaeda plan-

USA Today, "It's the Policies—Not Just the Place—That Matters," June 17, 2005. Copyright 2005 *USA Today*. Reproduced by permission.

ning, Osama bin Laden's bodyguards and 22 suspected terrorists abroad, according to [former] Defense Secretary Donald Rumsfeld.

- Moazzam Begg is a British citizen held at Guantanamo for three years before he was released [in 2005] without being charged. Begg and three other Britons freed at the same time have become international celebrities; their tales of unlawful detention and alleged mistreatment are known throughout the Muslim world.

Al-Kahtani's case represents the promise of intelligence gathering that led to Guantanamo's construction after the 9/11 attacks; Begg's case undermines the war on terrorism by convincing Muslims that the U.S. commitment to justice and human rights is hollow.

A Symbol of Hypocrisy

What to do about the facility is a question that transcends the facile "shut it down/keep it open" debates of recent weeks, or simplistic photo-ops of the chicken dinners served to detainees. It's a question of ends and means, perception and reality, and, ultimately, what the USA stands for.

Deservedly or not, in much of the world Guantanamo has grown into a symbol of U.S. hypocrisy. While lecturing other nations on democratic values, the United States keeps 520 mostly unidentified foreigners locked up on an isolated beachfront. Detainees are given meager legal resources to challenge their imprisonment. "It's our position that, legally, they can be held in perpetuity," Justice Department official J. Michael Wiggins told a Senate committee Wednesday [June 15, 2005].

Mixing the hypocrisy with steady drips of prisoner-abuse charges—al-Kahtani was literally treated like a dog, according to a *Time* magazine report—makes for a lethal cocktail that allows radicals to assert that the war on terror is a war on Islam. That was clear [in May 2005] when deadly riots erupted in Asia and the Middle East following a report in *Newsweek* that Guantanamo interrogators abused the Koran.

Closing Guantanamo ... wouldn't solve the perception problem.

Although the Koran-down-the-toilet report was discredited, it's indisputable that what started three years ago as an interrogation warehouse for fighters scraped off foreign battlefields, mainly in Afghanistan, has morphed into a public relations nightmare in the battle for hearts and minds in the Muslim world. If that battle is lost, so too will the war on terrorism.

Undercutting U.S. Values

Guantanamo is no Soviet-style gulag, as Amnesty International recently suggested, but the image problem has reached the point where senators of both parties, and former president Jimmy Carter, have called for closing it down. President [George W.] Bush seemed ... [in June 2005] to leave the door ajar to that possibility, but Rumsfeld and Vice President [Dick] Cheney rushed ... to slam it shut.

Those erratic policies, which have left the detainees in a legal black hole, have thwarted the key strategy in the United States' war on terror: leading with its values. Values that include rule of law. And opposition to torture.

The 9/11 Commission spelled out the components of a value-drenched strategy: Offer moral leadership to the world. Make the United States stand for a better future for Muslim youth. Join other nations to forge widely accepted agreements on how terror detainees should be treated.

Anyone stepping foot off U.S. shores knows the nation is losing that values campaign. Badly. Reporters traveling in Asia and the Middle East bring back stories describing how Guantanamo has seeped into the popular cultures there as a symbol of U.S. arrogance and lawlessness.

Closing Guantanamo and recreating some version of it elsewhere wouldn't solve the perception problem, but major changes in the way detainees are treated and processed could be a start.

Reveal the Identity and Treatment of Prisoners

Begin with radical transparency: Disclose who these detainees are, why they're being held and why they can't be returned to face charges in their home nations. Most important, open a discussion with allies on who should be designated "illegal combatants" in an era of terrorism that the Geneva Conventions [which set the standards for international humanitarian law] did not contemplate, and how they should be treated.

Finally, deal openly with the abuse claims. The White House says al-Qaeda trains its operatives to invent abuse allegations. No doubt. But the steady trickle of disturbing stories filtering out of Guantanamo, combined with the very real abuses found at prisons in Iraq and Afghanistan, suggests that some of the allegations have substance.

After more than three years [since the war began in Afghanistan in 2001], it's doubtful that many of those swept off the battlefield in Afghanistan have timely intelligence value.

If a campaign of radical transparency pares the 520 detainees at Guantanamo down to a handful deemed too dangerous to be released or returned to their home countries, then a corner will have been turned.

What matters most isn't whether that handful is housed in Cuba or elsewhere. What matters is that the United States turn to a broader campaign of leading with its values as well as its firepower.

10

American Public Support for the War on Terror Is Waning

Economist

The Economist *is a British news journal that focuses on international politics, business news, and opinion. Its articles are written anonymously to give the magazine a collective, unified voice.*

Public opinion polls in the United States have shown that support for the war in Iraq and the broader war on terror is flagging. The turn in sentiment may be due to increasing military casualties; reports of maltreatment of prisoners held at Guantanamo Bay, Cuba; and the government's overly optimistic assessments of America's achievements. Nonetheless, the majority of the public is likely to continue to support the war or at least not oppose it if the people believe the country is making progress. If this belief cannot be sustained, though, then the government could suffer a more detrimental loss of public confidence.

The war in Iraq has usually made comparisons with Vietnam look foolish. When it began, the word "quagmire" was barely out of critics' mouths before American troops were marching confidently into Baghdad [the capital of Iraq].

Now the Vietnam analogy is returning to haunt debate once again. Between one-third of Americans (in a poll by the Pew Research Centre) and almost half (in one for ABC) say Iraq will turn out to be another Vietnam. That is less than those who think America will avoid a quagmire, but a lot more than last year, when people decisively rejected the Vietnam analogy.

Surveys of Public Opinion on the War in Iraq

These lurid fears reflect a genuine turn in public opinion. [In June 2005], a Gallup poll found that 56% of people said it was not worth going to war—the lowest level of support since the invasion in 2003. Disapproval rates for President George Bush's conduct of the war have reached new peaks. The Pew survey found that almost as many people want troops to come home as want them to stay until the situation stabilises (46% to 50%: a tie, given the margin of error). For the first time, more than half the population thinks the war has not contributed to American security.

It is possible to claim—as the administration does—that these trends do not amount to a decisive turn in public opinion against the war. People are uneasy, the argument goes, but not defeatist. Their unease causes their views to fluctuate wildly in response to shortlived bad news.

There is some truth to this. Seventy-seven Americans were killed in May [2005], making it the fifth deadliest month since war began in March 2003. But if news from the front should start to improve, opinion will change rapidly.

The administration itself has probably worsened public unease with its own optimism. Mr Bush hailed the election in Iraq as "a great and historic achievement", which it was, but said rather less about the problems the new government would inherit. When civilian casualties soared, reaction set in. The president may perhaps be forgiven for his comment, but there seems little excuse for the remark at the end of May (a time of massive car bombs) by the vice-president, Dick Cheney, that the insurgency was in its "last throes". The administration's pattern of overselling achievements—remember "Mission accomplished"?—has probably made public opinion more nervous and volatile than it would otherwise be.

Guantanamo's Negative Image

Arguments over the mistreatment of prisoners in Guantanamo Bay may have further depressed opinion by raising questions about the essential rightness of America's behaviour in the war on terror. In late May, the secretary-general of Amnesty International compared the detention centre in Cuba with a Soviet gulag. Mr Bush called the analogy "absurd" (which it was: the gulags were essential to the operation of the Soviet state). But the charge still caused something of a rift in the Republican coalition.

The turn in [public] opinion is taking place in people's heads, not their hearts.

Mr Cheney said there was no plan to close the camp and insisted that "the important thing to understand is that the [prisoners] are bad people." But two Republican senators, Chuck Hagel of Nebraska and Mel Martinez of Florida, both argued that the facility may be more trouble than it is worth. Mr Martinez's comment ("At some point you wonder about the cost-benefit ratio") is especially striking considering his background: he was a member of the administration, and ran for the Senate with the encouragement of the White House. He is no Republican maverick wandering about off the reservation.

Stories of prisoner abuse would really make a difference, though, if they significantly dented Americans' image of themselves as the good guys abroad. So far, they have not done that. By a wide margin, people believe the reports are isolated incidents, not part of a wider pattern. This division is partisan. Liberal Democrats believe there is a wider pattern; everyone else thinks they are isolated incidents.

Dwindling Public Opinion
May Not Affect the War

So it is notable that while a clear majority is worried about the war, Americans are more evenly split on whether it was the right thing to do in the first place. Even now, slightly more people think the decision was right than wrong (though the majority is dwindling). That suggests there are reservoirs of support.

The administration can further claim that, despite all the wobbles, people essentially made up their minds about Iraq during the election campaign last year, and have not changed them since. The Pew poll provides intriguing evidence that this may be true. The centre asked respondents whether they were more or less emotionally involved in news about the war. The number of those saying they feel less involved has risen sharply. The turn in opinion is taking place in people's heads, not their hearts.

Lastly, the decline in support could be explained away as part of a wider outbreak of second-term blues. The president's job-approval ratings are miserable. Congress's are worse. The best indicator of political chirpiness—the question, "Do you think things are on the right or wrong track?"—is far below what it was after September 11th [2001] or during most of the late 1990s. Opinion on Iraq reflects, as well as contributes to, the malaise.

For all these reasons, it seems unlikely that the change in public opinion will cause any fundamental reappraisal of the administration's Iraq policy. And, of course, that would be extremely unlikely anyway. Mr Bush has staked his presidency on success in Iraq. It would take a huge backlash to force him to accept anything that smacks of failure or defeat, and the decline in public support is nowhere near strong enough to make him contemplate such a course.

Belief in Progress Sustains Public Support

But if the White House thinks this situation is sustainable—that it ploughs steadily on while public support bounces around—it is taking a big risk. Yes, opinion on Iraq bobbles around each month. But, argues Christopher Gelpi, a professor at Duke University [in North Carolina], the most important single factor determining the level of support is Americans' belief that they are winning. As long as they think they are, they will accept heavy casualties, and even discount torture as part of the price that must be paid.

This was true in Vietnam: opinion did not turn against that war until the Tet offensive in 1968, which was seen by the public as a defeat. Iraq has followed suit.

America's death toll passed 1,000 last September [2004], and this received a lot of coverage in the country. November [2004] was the bloodiest month since the war began, with a spate of insurgent attacks. Yet during this period, support for the Iraq policy rose slightly—because Americans were looking ahead to the elections in January and believed their country was making progress towards that goal, despite the level of violence. This summer [2005], the pattern has been the opposite. Iraq seems to be in political stalemate, nobody knows how to bring the Sunnis [one sect of Muslims] into the constitutional process—and support has fallen, even though the American death rate is lower than it was a few months earlier.

All this points to two dangers for the administration. First, by overselling the progress it has made, it risks reducing voters' patience in the face of inevitable setbacks. Second (and most important), public support depends critically on progress actually being made—which at the moment, it does not seem to be.

11

The U.S. Military-Industrial Complex Wants the War on Terror to Continue

Manuel Valenzuela

Manuel Valenzuela is an attorney, consultant, and freelance writer.

In 1961 President Dwight Eisenhower warned that a military-industrial complex was leading America down a path of increased militarism. Indeed, the U.S. purveyors of weapons and military technology have since tied themselves to the government, acquiring billions of dollars in contracts to arm the nation's military (and foreign militaries) while gaining positions of influence in the government offices that determine foreign policy. The combination has had tragic consequences; it has prompted America to seek war instead of peace so that the weapons trade may continue indefinitely. The current war on terror is simply the newest manifestation of the nation's militaristic foreign policy as orchestrated by the military-industrial complex. The armament industry wants this war, like the ones before it, to progress without victory to ensure profits continue unabated.

In the councils of government, we must guard against the acquisition of unwarranted influence, whether sought or unsought, by the military-industrial complex. The potential for the disastrous rise of misplaced power exists and will persist.

We must never let the weight of this combination endanger our liberties or democratic processes. We should take noth-

Manuel Valenzuela, "Perpetual War, Perpetual Terror," *Briarpatch*, vol. 33, October 2004. Copyright © 2004 *Briarpatch*, Inc. Reproduced by permission.

ing for granted. Only an alert and knowledgeable citizenry can compel the proper meshing of the huge industrial and military machinery of defense with our peaceful methods and goals, so that security and liberty may prosper together.

—Dwight D. Eisenhower, 1961

In the United States [in 2003] there were over 11,000 deaths by firearms. No other nation comes even close to matching this appetite for death. That is 8,000 more than died on 9/11 [September 11, 2001], but about the same number as those innocent Iraqi civilians that perished by our actions in Gulf War II [begun in 2003]. And the costs to American society from injuries and death due to firearms is more than $60 billion (USA). Those who produce instruments of death are not ignorant, however; they know the statistics, they simply brush them aside. Profit, after all, is much more important than stopping Americans from arming themselves to the teeth and killing each other. What else explains the gun lobby's attempts to go against common sense? The Second Amendment (right to keep and bear arms) must be honored and preserved, they say, even if the Founding Fathers never imagined the killing power of today's firearms. It is no coincidence, then, that the same nation that allows so many of its citizens to die at the hands of loaded weapons would naturally export its appetite for human death abroad.

The Death Industry

Today the USA is responsible for 40 percent of all worldwide weapons' sales. Tanks, fighter jets, artillery, helicopters, missiles, landmines, machine guns, mortars, bullets, grenades, guns, you name it, Guns'R'U.S. has it. Our nation supplies the world in instruments of death.

The United States' Military Industrial Complex (MIC) makes a killing from death, suffering and destruction. It exists only if people die. Its signature is everywhere; in the millions of landmines buried worldwide and the millions of amputee victims, many of them children. It can be seen in civil wars that ravage the world, from Africa to Asia to Latin America. From sea to shining sea, our weapons we can see, from the exponentially growing threat of weapons of mass destruction (WMDs)—many of which were distributed at one time by our own government—to the military hardware of tyrants, dictators, war criminals and warlords.

> The [military industrial complex] has embedded itself into the military branch of the USA government.

The MIC's front for assuring continual human violence is the USA government, the Pentagon in particular. President [George W.] Bush has granted the Pentagon a military budget of $400 billion for the [2005] fiscal year. That's $400,000,000,000.00 (USA). This, of course, does not include our little warmongering expedition to the Fertile Crescent, which by last estimates had already cost an additional $160 billion more. With so much of our money going to the "Department of War," one has to wonder where our priorities are. Certainly not in education, healthcare or in the creation of jobs.

The Government Abets the Military-Industrial Complex

The Pentagon and the Military Industrial Complex are one and the same, having morphed over time to form the most lethal killing institution the world has ever seen. Through a sliding and revolving door that turns citizen soldiers into armament industry executives and company officers into military policy makers, the MIC has embedded itself into the military branch of the USA government, thereby assuring itself of unlimited contracts, access, information and profit. Military industry executives and lobbyists have also slithered deep into top administration positions, occupying vitally important posts that decide national and foreign policy. Top government officials now sit on boards of today's biggest suppliers of military might. One need only look to the Carlyle Group to find the marriage between government and the MIC. George Bush the First had until recently sat on the board of this powerful yet clandestine group. This intertwined dancing tango of cronyism is exactly what Dwight D. Eisenhower warned about in 1961. Like a virus, the MIC has spread itself throughout the hallways of the Pentagon, penetrating from top to bottom through the disease called greed. Now one and the same, the Pentagon and the MIC have a common interest, motive and ability to shape how funds are used and wars are waged.

The Pentagon is the Department of War, not Defense. It is in business to kill, kill and kill some more. Without war, violence and weapons there is no Pentagon. And so to survive, to remain a player, wars must be created, weapons must be allocated, profits must be made and the Military Industrial Complex must continue exporting and manufacturing violence and conflict throughout the globe. And, as always, in the great tradition of the United States, enemies must exist. Indians, English, Mexicans, Spanish, Nazis, Koreans, Communists and now the ever-ambiguous Terrorists.

We are programmed to see the world as a conflict between Us and Them.

Finding a New Enemy

When the Cold War came to an end, so too did the great profits of the MIC. Reductions in the Pentagon budget threatened the lifeblood of the industry; a new enemy had to be unearthed. There is no war, and hence no profit, without evildoers—without terrorists lurking at every corner, waiting patiently for the moment to strike, instilling fear into our lives, absorbing our attention.

We are told our nation is in imminent danger, that we are a mushroom cloud waiting to happen. And so we fear; transforming our mass uneasiness into nationalistic and patriotic fervor, wrapping ourselves up in the flag and the Military Industrial Complex. We have fallen into the trap and have become the subservient slaves of an engine run by greed, interested not in peace but constant war, constant killing and constant sacrifice to the almighty dollar. Brainwashed to believe that War is Peace we sound the drums of war, marching our sons and daughters to a battle that cannot be won by sword or gun.

We are programmed to see the world as a conflict between Us and Them, or Good versus Evil, and we must inflict death on those who are not with us and on those against us. The MIC preys on our human emotions and psychology, exploiting our still fragile memories of the horrors of 9/11, manipulating us to believe that what they say and do is right for us all. We unite against the enemy, fearing for our lives, complacent and obedient, blindly descending like a plague of locusts onto foreign land, devastating, usurping, conquering and devouring those who have been deemed enemies of the state, those who harbour and live among them, "evil ones" and "evildoers" and "haters of freedom," all for the sake of profit and pillage, ideology and empire.

A War Without End

The so-called "War on Terror" is but a charade; a fear-engendering escapade, designed to last into perpetuity, helping guarantee that the Military Industrial Complex will grow exponentially in power. It is a replacement for a Cold War long ago retired, unable to deliver a massive increase in defense spending. Terrorists and the countries that harbor them have replaced the Soviet Union and Communists as enemy number one. With a war that may go on indefinitely, pursuing an enemy that lives in shadows and in the haze of ambiguity, the

MIC will grow ever more powerful, conscripting hundreds of thousands of our youth, sending them to guide, operate and unleash their products of death.

Rumblings of bringing back the draft are growing louder, and if you think your children and grandchildren will escape it, think again. In a war without end, in battles that do not cease, the MIC will need fresh human flesh to replace those who perish and fall wounded. Empire building needs bodies and drones to go with military might; instruments of death need trigger fingers and human brains. In this so-called "war on terror" the MIC will continue its reprogramming of expendable young men and women from peaceful civilians to warmongering killing machines. After all, "War is Peace."

We are becoming that which we fear the most, a terrorist state.

A perpetual war is what the MIC has sought all along. A lifetime of combat, a lifetime of profit, a lifetime of power. Assembly lines of missiles, bombs, tanks and aircraft operate without pause, helping expand a sluggish economy and the interests of the Pax Americana. Profit over people, violence before peace, the American killing machine continues on its path to human extinction, and it is the hands and minds of our best and brightest building and creating these products of decimation.

An Aggressive Posture That Invites Resentment

While we look over our shoulders for terrorists and evildoers, the world ominously looks directly at us, not knowing on which nation the storm of satellite-guided missiles will rain down on next. Every action has an equal and opposite reaction. In becoming preemptive warmongers, we are also becoming victims of our own making, helping assure a swelling wrath of revenge, resentment and retaliation against us. If we kill we will be killed, if we destroy we will be destroyed. The MIC is leading us down a steep canyon of fury, making us a pariah, a rogue country in the eyes of the world. We are becoming that which we fear most, a terrorist state.

As political scientist and ex-marine C. Douglas Lummis has said, "Air bombardment is state terrorism, the terrorism of the rich. It has burned up and blasted apart more innocents in the past six decades than have all the anti-state terrorists who have ever lived. Something has benumbed our consciousness against this reality." Today we are seen, along with Israel, as the greatest threats to world peace. When hundreds of thousands throughout the planet call Bush "the world's number one terrorist," that less than admirable distinction is automatically imputed onto the nation as a whole and the citizens in particular. This can be seen in the world's perception and treatment of us today.

When the day comes, not too far in the future, when one of our cities goes up in a mushroom cloud or in a vapor of suffocation, or when tens of thousands of citizens die of biological or chemical demons, we must dive deep into our national psyche and question why we allowed those in power to guide us down the road of cause and effect, action and reaction. And, in the end, we must realize that those same WMDs we once so gleefully created and exported have come back to our shores, haunting us and our children for the suffering we have helped spread throughout the world through our idleness; impotence to act and automaton-like acquiescence.

The Potential to Change

Can you imagine spending $400 billion to alleviate poverty in the Middle East? Can you imagine spending $400 billion to improve the lives of millions who today have nothing to live for, except martyrdom? Wouldn't $400 billion go further than perpetual bloodshed in the insidious war on terror if we alleviated the suffering and poverty of the world's poor by helping to provide jobs, education and medicines which would in turn spawn a sense of goodwill towards the USA?

Could it be remotely possible that our foreign policy, our support for puppet dictators and monarchs, our quest for empire and resources and our unyielding military, financial and political support of the dehumanization of the Palestinian people by Israel all leads to the subjugation, injustice, humiliation and misery of hundreds of millions of people? Could this be why we are so hated throughout a world where billions have nothing while we bathe in abundance—the spoils of war? As long as the MIC acts in our name while plundering humanity, we will be hated. [Indian pacifist Mohandas K.] Gandhi once said that "an eye for an eye only leads to more blindness." If that is so, then our nation is on a collision course with an ominous black hole whose darkness we shall not escape and whose exit we will never again see. Unless. . . .

12

The War on Terror Is Increasing Militarism Around the Globe

Matthew O'Rourke

Matthew O'Rourke is a member of Project Ploughshares, an agency of the Canadian Council of Churches. Its mission is to provide analysis on and help shape church response to issues of conflict and peace worldwide. O'Rourke's work will involve researching and documenting areas of armed conflict worldwide.

The war on terror was supposedly undertaken to bring security to the world's nations. Ironically, the war has increased military spending in the United States and spread U.S. military assistance to several conflict-ridden parts of the world. The result has been to intensify regional conflicts and, in some cases, to involve the U.S. military in nationalist conflicts that have inappropriately been labeled antiterrorism campaigns.

The wars in Iraq and Afghanistan would not exist in their current form were it not for the US-led campaign against terrorism. Indeed, the effects of the fight to stop international terrorism have been felt in many of the intra-state conflicts identified in Project Ploughshares' annual Armed Conflicts Report (ACR). Although it is far too early to draw any solid conclusions about the impact of the campaign on terrorism, several important trends appear to be developing.

Economic Impact

The war on terror has had two major economic impacts so far:

- An increase in overall military assistance to countries experiencing conflict.

- The elimination of sanctions on arms exports to these countries.

Although many countries are participating in the fight against terrorism, the US is very much in the lead and will be the focus of this analysis. Increased military assistance comes primarily from the US, in two main forms:

- Foreign Military Financing (FMF)—congressionally appropriated grants to foreign governments to help finance the purchase of American weapons, services, and training;

- International Military Education and Training (IMET) grants, which are given to foreign governments to pay for training by US military personnel on US weapons systems. Since 11 September 2001 the focus of IMET has been on counter-terrorism training.

Increases in military funding since 2001 to countries experiencing conflict vary greatly, as do their effects. Pakistan, Nepal, Algeria, Chad, the Philippines, Colombia, Kenya, India, Indonesia, Serbia and Montenegro, Nigeria, Uganda, Senegal, and Ethiopia have all experienced either an increase in US military assistance or the elimination of sanctions that prevented their buying US arms. Although countries such as Kenya and Indonesia have experienced small increases in funding that may not have a significant long-term impact on the country or conflict, others, like Pakistan, have experienced huge increases in military assistance that are likely to have serious long-term effects.

In a very short time Pakistan has changed from a country under severe US sanctions and military restrictions to one of the largest beneficiaries of US military assistance in the world. Between 1999 and 2001, Pakistan received only $174,000 in IMET and no FMF at all. In 2002, Pakistan received no IMET funding but received $75,000,000 in FMF. In 2003, US military assistance rose to over $200,000,000, and while it dropped to $75,000,000 in 2004, the US administration has requested over $300,000,000 for Pakistan in 2005, even though the US Department of State (2005) describes Pakistan's human rights record as poor. Although the impact of this financing is not yet clear, funding could potentially affect both internal conflict within Pakistan as well as Pakistan's involvement in wars in Afghanistan and Kashmir.

In late January of 2004, the US Congress approved a $574,600,000 military aid package to Colombia.

Nepal has also experienced an increase in US military assistance. In 2000 and 2001, Nepal received under $250,000 per year in US military assistance. Despite the fact that Nepal is currently experiencing one of the world's most violent and deadly conflicts, is described by the US State Department as having a poor human rights record, and has state security forces committing "numerous serious abuses," US military assistance rose to over $17,000,000 in 2002. In 2003 the US Administration requested $9,500,000 for military aid to Nepal, and in 2004 $16,600,000.

Colombia and the Philippines have felt the financial impact of the international fight against terrorism. While US military assistance has not risen to previous high levels, it has increased somewhat since 2001. In late January of 2004, the US Congress approved a $574,600,000 military aid package to Colombia, despite the fact that, once again, the State Department labeled Colombia's human rights record as poor. (In

2005, the State Department noted some improvements in the record, although there are still serious problems.) In May 2003, the US committed more than $114,000,000 in military aid to help defeat terrorists in the Philippines. This was the largest US military assistance package since the US closed its Philippine bases in 1992.

Political Impact

The campaign against terrorism has had political, as well as economic, repercussions. There has been a concerted effort to link conflicts to the terrorist attacks of September 11 and to reclassify opposition and rebel groups as "terrorists." Once rebel groups are classified as terrorists, governments feel less pressure to negotiate and become less willing to enter into a peace process. In many cases this disinclination towards negotiation leads a government to seek a military victory through the extermination of the rebel group. As well, links between rebel groups and international terrorist organizations, whether proven or not, are emphasized to isolate the groups and to justify a refusal to negotiate with them. Once a group is labeled "terrorist," its grievances, legitimate or not, are usually viewed as invalid, reducing international pressure on governments to work towards a negotiated settlement. And identifying an opposition group as "terrorists" helps a country obtain funding from the US as part of the war on terror. While this increase in funding may eventually lead to a military victory, it immediately intensifies ongoing conflicts.

In Russia, for example, a link has been made between the September 11 attacks and the war in Chechnya. On 12 September 2004, Russian President Vladimir Putin formally linked the war in Chechnya to the attacks on the World Trade Center towers and the Pentagon by declaring that Russia and the US had a "common foe." Putin alleged links between Chechen rebels and [Osama] Bin Laden's al Qaeda terrorist network.

Following this speech by Putin, both US and EU [European Union] criticisms of the Kremlin's handling of the war in Chechnya softened.

The Communist Party of Nepal is now on the US State Department's list of terrorist organizations. This labeling has caused problems in negotiations between the government and the rebels.

In Colombia distinctions between the war on terror and the war on drugs have become blurry. Indeed, the blending of the two appeared complete in November 2004 when US President [George W.] Bush referred to Colombia's rebels and paramilitaries as "narco-terrorists." All the major Colombian rebel groups and paramilitaries are on the US State Department's list of terrorist organizations.

Occasionally the international fight against terrorism has led to the direct involvement of the US military in a [regional or civil] conflict.

All three of the main active rebel groups in the Philippines are on the US State Department's list of terrorist organizations. Peace processes between the government and the Communist Party of the Philippines/National People's Army (CPP/NPA) have been put on hold indefinitely because of the terrorist labeling. Since rumours arose of links between Jamaah Islamiya (an Islamic terrorist organization based in the Philippines, also on the list of terrorist organizations) and the Moro Islamic Liberation Front (MILF), the Philippine government has refused to negotiate with MILF. The third group, Abu Sayyaf, which was once viewed by the Philippine government as a "criminal network" because of their involvement in kidnapping and ransom, now features prominently on the list of terrorist organizations and is a main target in the fight against international terrorism.

Direct U.S. Military Involvement

Occasionally the international fight against terrorism has led to the direct involvement of the US military in a conflict. Recently the US has become more active in Colombia, doubling its troop commitment, increasing its annual aid package to over $570-million, and sending an additional 200 civilian contract personnel to Colombia. The US also indicted and issued extradition warrants for 23 members of rebel and paramilitary forces on drug and terrorism charges. The US interfered with a planned major prisoner exchange with rebel groups by stating that if Colombia released the prisoners in order to exchange them, the US would press charges and ask for them to be extradited.

The US is heavily involved in the battle with Abu Sayyaf. In January 2002, the US sent 600 soldiers to support 4,000 Philippine troops in a major operation against Abu Sayyaf in the south. With the new influx of money and the Philippine government's refusal to negotiate with "terrorists," it seems likely that the conflict in the Philippines will escalate. Several African countries are also experiencing direct US involvement in large counter-terrorism programs. The Pan-Sahel Initiative, now known as the Trans-Sahara Counter-Terrorism Initiative, was established in 2002 and is based in Djibouti. Between 1,200 and 1,500 US marines are training security personnel in a number of African countries. This initiative has a budget in the millions.

Chad is part of this initiative. With US funding and assistance, the Chadian military's basic training has undergone a major change. In the past, during basic training each Chadian soldier shot just eight bullets, but those trained by the US in 2004 shot over 122,000 bullets each. The Chadian military also received new US uniforms and 13 new Toyota pickup trucks. With the aid of a US surveillance plane in March 2004, Chadian troops pursued and killed 42 fighters in the north of Chad.

The US-led campaign to combat international terrorism is influencing armed conflicts around the world. Close attention must be paid to the broader impacts of the war on terror to understand the implications in different parts of the world.

13

America Cannot Win the War Against Terrorism by Giving in to Hatred

Gerald Leonard Spence

Gerald (Gerry) Leonard Spence is a trial lawyer and founder of the Trial Lawyers College. His legal expertise has made him a well-regarded television commentator. Spence is also the author of several books.

The terrorists who attacked America on September 11, 2001 were motivated by hate. America has unlimited power to respond to this hatred, but unfortunately those in control of that power wish only to respond in kind. This will only lead to more tragedies and do nothing to address the spirit of hatred that lies within America's enemies. Instead, Americans must guard against the savage use of power and stick to its values by upholding the rule of law. Only by being a beacon of lawful freedom can the United States overcome the forces of hatred.

I am terror stricken. I am having a nightmare in which the United States has been defeated, its people enslaved, its freedoms confiscated, and its citizens imprisoned within their own borders. I awaken to discover that the dream could be true.

The enemy, of course, is Hatred. And Power—even absolute power—cannot destroy Hatred. Power can only create Hatred.

Gerald Leonard Spence, "Have We Already Been Defeated?" *The Humanist*, vol. 62, March–April 2002. Copyright © 2002 American Humanist Association. Reproduced by permission of the author.

Hatred killed thousands in New York City and instantly created 260 million people filled with rage and a new hatred of their own. The giant can kill terrorist leaders and those who succor them. The giant can wipe out their villages. But Hatred will find ways to obliterate our freedoms, our institutions, to extinguish our moral beacons and at last it may even destroy our cities and civilization.

Power can win the body count but it can't win this war. Because the enemy is not human. This is a war against a malicious spirit. Only fools attempt to defeat a spirit with guns and rockets and bombs. It is like blowing up the air. It is like bombing graveyards. Some have said this is a war of good against evil. But power that only begets hatred is not good, and in the end hatred becomes the most indomitable power of all.

Giving in to Hatred

Already the United States has committed our children to kill and be killed. Meanwhile, the enemy—Hatred—laughs, because it knows that killing on either side will bring on more hatred until, after decades, perhaps generations, the giant will have depleted itself, its coffers drained, its natural resources exhausted, its population drowned in fear and sorrow and hatred over the endless fields of dead.

I speak here of a simple proposition—one that people of power find difficult to understand because people of power understand only power. They play to an inflamed and suffering people often without asking careful questions, expressing hatred instead. Reason is out. Dissent is deemed unpatriotic. To ask a simple question like, "Why are we hated so?" cannot be answered. Justice has become confused with killing so that the more we kill in retribution, and the sooner, the more justice we are said to receive. But such justice delivers only hatred—theirs and ours.

Let us go forward to that time when the body count is over. We can see their dead and ours lined in long rows; the parts of their bodies in terrible heaps; the mangled and limbless children; the weeping, the wounded, and the wretched. No longer can we trust our neighbors. No longer can we wander safely from our own borders or move within them without fear.

Our Constitution is only a shredded memory on faded parchment. We cannot speak freely for fear we will be hated. Our civil liberties, once guaranteed under that blessed document, have given way to the exigencies of this struggle. The police have demanded that they be given more power, that they be permitted to tap our phones and search our homes without warrants. We have become prisoners with electronic tattoos. Reacting to our fear we have embraced the police who have promised to keep us safe. But we are no longer safe from them and the courts turn their heads.

That blessed ideal fundamental to any free nation—the rule of law—can no longer be heard through the racket of our rage. Hatred also hates freedom and despises the rule of law. Once the rule of law has been forfeited, like an arm severed, like a leg amputated, like a soul stripped of its sense of humanity, it can never again be called upon to protect a free people.

We ... must ensure that unleashed Power ... doesn't itself become the most proficient, the most hideous ... terrorist in the history of humanity.

Maintaining the Rule of Law

The goal of a free nation must be no different outside its borders than within them. In the United States we don't massacre whole towns because they may be the chosen domicile of a criminal or a conspiracy of criminals. Instead we carefully root out the felons and bring them to justice.

If we ask, indeed, to remain a free nation, we, the people, must ensure that unleashed Power—this enraged giant—doesn't itself become the most proficient, the most hideous, the most gargantuan terrorist in the history of humanity and thereby plant a crop that bears an eternal fruit of hatred.

We cannot be asked to love those who have wrought such pain and death on so many innocent people. Such love is beyond the capacity of the human organism. But through love of our system we can refuse to nourish Hatred and instead accept the greatest of challenges—indeed the greatest of opportunities—that have ever been tendered a free nation: to guide the world toward a day when we shall be free from fear and terrorism by embracing, yes, cherishing, the rule of law.

It is the majesty of the rule of law that underlies the Constitution of the United States. With it we can lead the world to freedom. Without it we are doomed to the endless pain and destruction that an unleashed Hatred will forever wage upon us. In a sane world, we can never surrender to that evil entity.

Organizations to Contact

The editors have compiled the following list of organizations concerned with the issues debated in this book. The descriptions are derived from materials provided by the organizations. All have publications or information available for interested readers. The list was compiled on the date of publication of the present volume; the information provided here may change. Be aware that many organizations take several weeks or longer to respond to inquiries, so allow as much time as possible.

American Civil Liberties Union (ACLU)
125 Broad St., 18th Fl., New York, NY   10004-2400
(212) 549-2500
e-mail: aclu@aclu.org
Web site: www.aclu.org

The ACLU is a national organization that works to defend Americans' civil rights. The ACLU argues that measures to protect national security in the wake of terrorist attacks should not compromise civil liberties. Its publications include "Civil Liberties After 9-11: The ACLU Defends Freedom" and "National ID Cards: 5 Reasons Why They Should Be Rejected."

American Enterprise Institute (AEI)
1150 Seventeenth St. NW, Washington, DC   20036
(202) 862-5800 • fax (202) 862-7177
Web site: www.aei.org

The AEI is a nonpartisan organization dedicated to researching and providing information concerning U.S. domestic and foreign policy. The institute focuses on issues such as economic policy, social and political studies, and defense policy. The AEI promotes democratization as a tool to win the war on terror. *American Enterprise* is the bimonthly magazine published by the institute, and many other publications are available on the group's Web site.

Brookings Institution
1775 Massachusetts Ave. NW, Washington, DC 20036
(202) 797-6240 • fax (202) 797-2970
e-mail: brookinfo@brookings.edu
Web site: www.brook.edu

The Brookings Institution conducts foreign policy research and analyzes global events and their impact on the United States. The institute's analysis of the war on terror suggests new tactics are needed to reduce the threat of terrorism. Policy briefs as well as analysis and commentary can be found on the Brookings Institution Web site.

Carnegie Endowment for International Peace
1779 Massachusetts Ave. NW, Washington, DC 20036-2103
(202) 483-7600 • fax (202) 483-1840
e-mail: info@CarnegieEndowment.org
Web site: www.carnegieendowment.org

The Carnegie Endowment for International Peace, a private, nonpartisan organization, supports strong U.S. foreign policy. The organization is critical, however, of the ways in which the United States has interacted with the world as a result of the war on terror and related foreign policies. The Carnegie Endowment publishes the bimonthly magazine *Foreign Policy* and has many other publications available on its Web site.

Cato Institute
1000 Massachusetts Ave. NW, Washington, DC 20001-5403
(202) 842-0200 • fax (202) 842-3490
Web site: www.cato.org

The Cato Institute, a libertarian research organization, uses Jeffersonian philosophy as the basis for much of its public policy analysis. The institute endorses the spread of American political values and the promotion of free-market systems. The organization contends, however, that the war on terror represents a failure in U.S. foreign policy. The *Cato Journal* is published triannually, coinciding with the conclusion of conferences held by the institute. Additional materials presenting viewpoints on all areas of public policy can be found on the group's Web site.

Center for American Progress
1333 H St. NW, 10th Fl., Washington, DC   20005
(202) 682-1611
e-mail: progress@americanprogress.org
Web site: www.americanprogress.org

The Center for American Progress is a nonpartisan institute that promotes a liberal, progressive agenda. Challenging conservative ideals provides the groundwork for the organization's analysis of U.S. policy. The Center for American Progress encourages a strong response in the fight against terrorism and the protection of America, but it also argues that a multilateral approach best supports America's interests. Numerous newsletters can be requested online from the center, covering topics such as national security, domestic policy, and economic policy.

Center for Strategic and International Studies (CSIS)
1800 K St. NW, Washington, DC   20006
(202) 887-0200 • fax: (202) 775-3199
Web site: www.csis.org

CSIS is a public policy research institution that focuses on America's economic policy, national security, and foreign and domestic policy. The center analyzes global crises and suggests U.S. military policies. Its publications include the journal *Washington Quarterly* and the studies "Protecting Against the Spread of Nuclear, Biological, and Chemical Weapons" and "Cyberthreats, Information Warfare, and Critical Infrastructure Protection: Defending the U.S. Homeland."

Council on Foreign Relations (CFR)
58 East 68th St., New York, NY   10021
(212) 434-9400 • fax (212) 434-9800
Web site: www.cfr.org

The CFR is a nonpartisan organization dedicated to providing information to further the public's understanding of international foreign policy. The CFR has provided extensive analysis of the war on terror, addressing everything from the definition of terrorism to the question of how much progress has been made. The CFR publishes the journal *Foreign Affairs*.

Heritage Foundation

214 Massachusetts Ave. NE, Washington, DC   20002-4999
(202) 546-4400 • fax (202) 546-8328
e-mail: info@heritage.org
Web site: www.heritage.org

The Heritage Foundation provides research and information on current public policies from the conservative point of view. The organization supports the war on terror, and it defines the war in Iraq as an important facet of defeating terrorism. The Heritage Foundation Web site provides numerous publications outlining the organization's stance on the fight against terrorism.

International Policy Institute for Counter-Terrorism (ICT)

PO Box 167, Herzlia   46150
   Israel
972-9-9527277 • fax: 972-9-9513073
e-mail: info@ict.org.il
Web site: www.ict.org.il

ICT is a research institute that develops public policy solutions to international terrorism. Its Web site is a comprehensive resource on terrorism and counterterrorism, including an extensive database on terrorist organizations. Numerous articles on terrorism are published on the Web site, including "The Continuing Al-Qaida Threat" and "The Changing Threat of International Terrorism."

Middle East Policy Council (MEPC)

1730 M St. NW, Suite 512, Washington, DC   20036
(202) 296-6767 • fax (202) 296-5791

e-mail: info@mepc.org
Web site: www.mepc.org

The MEPC encourages and facilitates discussion about U.S. government policies involving the Middle East. The organization criticizes the war on terror as being improperly defined and wrongly focused. *Middle East Policy* is the quarterly journal published by the MEPC, and the Web site of the council provides links to other information on the Middle East.

Peace Action
1100 Wayne Ave., Suite 1020, Silver Spring, MD   20910
(301) 565-4050 • fax (301) 565-0850
Web site: www.peace-action.org

Peace Action believes that war is not a viable option for conflict resolution and lobbies for U.S. foreign policy that does not employ preemptive war as a tool of diplomacy. Peace Action is currently calling for the withdrawal of American troops from Iraq.

United Nations Counter-Terrorism Committee (UN CTC)
140 East 45th St., New York, NY   10017
(212) 415-4050 • fax (212) 415-4053
e-mail: usunpublicaffairs@state.gov
Web site: www.un.org

The Security Council of the United Nations (UN) is the home of the CTC, an organization dedicated to defining the UN's actions against terrorism. The committee is comprised of the fifteen member nations of the Security Council, and has released strong statements condemning terrorism and pledging support to those who are working to fight its spread. Many resolutions, statements, and policy papers concerning terrorism are available on the organization's Web site.

U.S. Department of State Counterterrorism Office
Office of the Coordinator for Counterterrorism, Office of Public Affairs, Room 2509, Washington, DC   20520

(202) 647-4000
Web site: www.state.gov/s/ct

The U.S. Department of State is a federal agency that advises the president on foreign policy matters. The Office of Counterterrorism publishes the annual report *Patterns of Global Terrorism*, a list of the United States' most-wanted terrorists, and numerous fact sheets and press releases on the war on terrorism.

Washington Institute for Near East Policy
1828 L St. NW, Suite 1050, Washington, DC 20036
(202) 452-0650 • fax (202) 223-5364
Web site: http://washingtoninstitute.org

The Washington Institute for Near East Policy is dedicated to providing accurate, nonpartisan information to assist in the creation of U.S. policies concerning the Middle East. Many articles and topics pertaining to the war on terror are available on the group's Web site.

Bibliography

Books

Daniel Benjamin and Steven Simon   *The Next Attack: The Failure of the War on Terror and a Strategy for Getting It Right.* New York: Times Books, 2005.

Tony Blankley   *The West's Last Chance: Will We Win the Clash of Civilizations?* Washington, DC: Regnery, 2005.

Jane Boulden and Thomas G. Weiss, eds.   *Terrorism and the UN: Before and After September 11.* Bloomington: Indiana University Press, 2004.

Rachel Ehrenfeld   *Funding Evil: How Terrorism Is Financed—and How to Stop It.* Chicago: Bonus Books, 2003.

Richard Falk   *The Great Terror War.* New York: Olive Branch, 2003.

David Frum and Richard Perle   *An End to Evil: How to Win the War on Terror.* New York: Random House, 2003.

Mike Green   *The WHOLE Truth About the U.S. War on Terror.* Waldwick, NJ: NewMedia, 2005.

Stephen Hess and Marvin Kalb, eds.   *The Media and the War on Terrorism.* Washington, DC: Brookings Institution Press, 2003.

Ronald Kessler — *The CIA at War: Inside the Secret Campaign Against Terror.* New York: St. Martin's, 2003.

Walter Laqueur — *No End to War: Terrorism in the Twenty-First Century.* New York: Continuum, 2003.

Michael Ledeen — *The War Against the Terror Masters: Why It Happened, Where We Are Now, How We'll Win.* New York: St. Martin's, 2002.

Ian Lustick — *Trapped in the War on Terror.* Philadelphia: University of Pennsylvania Press, 2006.

Richard Miniter — *Shadow War: The Untold Story of How Bush Is Winning the War on Terror.* Washington, DC: Regnery, 2004.

Laurie Mylroie — *Bush vs. the Beltway: The Inside Battle over War in Iraq.* New York: Regan, 2003.

Michael Scheuer — *Imperial Hubris: Why the West Is Losing the War on Terror.* Dulles, VA: Potomac, 2004.

Gary Schroen — *First In: An Insider's Account of How the CIA Spearheaded the War on Terror in Afghanistan.* New York: Presidio, 2005.

William W. Turner — *Mission Not Accomplished: How George Bush Lost the War on Terrorism.* Roseville, CA: Penmarin, 2004.

Richard Ashby Wilson, ed. | *Human Rights in the "War on Terror."* New York: Cambridge University Press, 2005.

Periodicals

Andrew J. Bacevich | "This Is Not World War Three—or Four," *Spectator*, July 22, 2006.

Daniel Benjamin, Steven Simon, and Richard A. Falkenrath | "The War of Unintended Consequences," *Foreign Affairs*, March–April 2006.

Ferry Biedermann | "Winning the Battle Against Terror, Losing the War of Ideas," Salon.com, January 9, 2004. www.salon.com.

Max Boot | "It's Not Over Yet," *Time*, September 11, 2006.

David Brooks | "Trading Cricket for Jihad," *New York Times*, August 4, 2005.

Phillip Carter | "Tainted by Torture," *Slate*, May 14, 2004. www.slate.com.

Juan Cole | "9/11: The Attacks on the United States Were Neither a Clash of Civilizations Nor an Unqualified Success for al Qaeda. They Were, However, a Clash of Policy That Continues to This Day," *Foreign Policy*. September–October 2006.

Anthony H. Cordesman | "Saudi Arabia: Friend or Foe in the War on Terror?" *Middle East Policy*, Spring 2006.

Con Coughlin "To Solve the Afghan Crisis, Get Tough on Pakistan," *Spectator*, July 15, 2006.

Maureen Dowd "A Defense That's Offensively Weak," *New York Times*, March 10, 2005.

Economist "Why It Will Take So Long to Win," February 25, 2006.

Ivan Eland "It's What We Do: The Administration Says the Terrorists Hate Us for Who We Are. But That Isn't What the Terrorists Say—or What the Record Shows," *American Prospect*, January 2006.

Sandra I. Erwin "Defense Dept. Rhetoric Reflects War Frustrations," *National Defense*, September 2005.

Harold Evans "A Time to Stand Firm," *U.S. News & World Report*, July 18, 2005.

Bruce Fein "Between War and Peace," *Washington Times*, September 6, 2006.

Gerard P. Fogarty "Is Guantanamo Bay Undermining the Global War on Terror?" *Parameters*, Autumn 2005.

Graham E. Fuller "Strategic Fatigue," *National Interest*, Summer 2006.

John Heilemann   "George W. and the Dominoes: Iraq Was Supposed to Trigger a Democratic Chain Reaction in the Middle East. Instead—See the Missiles over Haifa—the Tumbling Is Going Backward," *New York*, August 14, 2006.

Lynda Hurst   "War on Terror Called a Failure," *Toronto Star*, June 15, 2006.

Michael Ignatieff   "Could We Lose the War on Terror? Lesser Evils," *New York Times Magazine*, May 2, 2004.

Seth G. Jones   "Don't Bomb Iran," *Record*, April 14, 2006.

William Kristol   "Victory in Spite of All Terror," *Weekly Standard*, July 18, 2005.

John Lehman   "We're Not Winning This War," *Washington Post*, August 31, 2006.

Andrew C. McCarthy   "Three Years and Counting: The U.S. Has Not Suffered a Major Attack Since September 2001. Why?" *National Review*, December 13, 2004.

Doyle McManus   "Is the U.S. Winning This War?" *Los Angeles Times*, September 10, 2006.

Joshua Muravchik   "Hearts, Minds, and the War Against Terror," *Commentary*, May 2002.

Jeremy Rabkin   "Not as Bad as You Think: The Court Hasn't Crippled the War on Terror," *Weekly Standard*, July 17, 2006.

Ahmed Rashid — "Who's Winning the War on Terror?" *Yale Global*, September 5, 2003.

Tom Regan — "Experts: U.S. Must Win 'War of Ideas,'" *Christian Science Monitor*, June 16, 2006.

David B. Rivkin and Lee A. Casey — "Unwarranted Complaints," *New York Times*, December 27, 2005.

John Robb — "The Open-Source War," *New York Times*, October 15, 2005.

Daniel Schulman — "Mind Games: Information Has Always Been a Weapon. But in the Amorphous 'War on Terror,' Bombs and Bullets Are Becoming Background Noise in the Battle to Frame Reality," *Columbia Journalism Review*, May–June 2006.

John L. Sherer — "The U.S.'s Befuddled Approach to the War on Terrorism," *USA Today Magazine*, November 2004.

Robert Wright — "Terror in the Past and Future Tense," *New York Times*, April 26, 2005.

Fareed Zakaria — "Mao & Stalin, Osama & Saddam; Bush Is Starting to Repeat One of the Central Errors of the Cold War; Treating Our Enemies as One Entity," *Newsweek International*, September 18, 2006.

Mortimer B. Zuckerman — "We Can Win—and We Must," *U.S. News & World Report*, September 13, 2004.

Index